The Hidden History of Big Brother in America

INDEX

THE
HIDDEN HISTORY *of*
BIG BROTHER IN AMERICA

HOW THE DEATH OF
PRIVACY AND THE RISE OF
SURVEILLANCE THREATEN
US AND OUR DEMOCRACY

THOM HARTMANN

Berrett–Koehler Publishers, Inc.

Berrett-Koehler Publishers, Inc.
1333 Broadway, Suite 1000
Oakland, CA 94612-1921
Tel: (510) 817-2277; Fax: (510) 817-2278
www.bkconnection.com

ORDERING INFORMATION
Quantity sales. Special discounts are available on quantity purchases by corporations, associations, and others. For details, contact the "Special Sales Department" at the Berrett-Koehler address above.
Individual sales. Berrett-Koehler publications are available through most bookstores. They can also be ordered directly from Berrett-Koehler: Tel: (800) 929-2929; Fax: (802) 864-7626; www.bkconnection.com.
Orders for college textbook / course adoption use. Please contact Berrett-Koehler: Tel: (800) 929-2929; Fax: (802) 864-7626.

Distributed to the U.S. trade and internationally by Penguin Random House Publisher Services.

Berrett-Koehler and the BK logo are registered trademarks of Berrett-Koehler Publishers, Inc.

Printed in the United States of America

Berrett-Koehler books are printed on long-lasting acid-free paper. When it is available, we choose paper that has been manufactured by environmentally responsible processes. These may include using trees grown in sustainable forests, incorporating recycled paper, minimizing chlorine in bleaching, or recycling the energy produced at the paper mill.

Library of Congress Cataloging-in-Publication Data
Names: Hartmann, Thom, 1951– author.
Title: The hidden history of big brother in America : how the death of privacy and the rise of surveillance threaten us and our democracy / Thom Hartmann.
Description: First edition | Oakland : Berrett-Koehler, 2022. | Includes bibliographical references and index.
Identifiers: LCCN 2021034448 (print) | LCCN 2021034449 (ebook) | ISBN 9781523001026 (paperback) | ISBN 9781523001033 (adobe pdf) | ISBN 9781523001040 (epub)
Subjects: LCSH: Privacy, Right of—Political aspects—United States. | Data protection—Law and legislation—United States. | Electronic surveillance—Law and legislation—United States. | Social media—Law and legislation—United States. | Social control—United States. | United States—Politics and government.
Classification: LCC KF1263.C65 . H375 2022 (print) | LCC KF1263.C65 (ebook) | DDC 342.7308/58—dc23
LC record available at https://lccn.loc.gov/2021034448
LC ebook record available at https://lccn.loc.gov/2021034449

First Edition
28 27 26 25 24 23 22   10 9 8 7 6 5 4 3 2 1

Book production: Linda Jupiter Productions   *Cover design:* Wes Youssi, M.80 Design
Edit: Elissa Rabellino   *Interior design:* Good Morning Graphics
Proofread: Mary Kanable   *Index:* Leiser Indexing

*To George DiCaprio, Leonardo DiCaprio, Leila Connors,
Roee Sharon Peled, and Earl Katz, dear friends with whom I've
been honored to make some great media and whose
positive impacts on the world will echo for generations.*

Quis custodiet ipsos custodes?
("Who watches the watchers?")

—Juvenal, first-century Roman satirist

CONTENTS

The Big Picture of Social Control vs. Democracy

"Without the right of privacy, there is no real freedom of speech or freedom of opinion, and so there is no actual democracy."
—**Dilma Rousseff, former President of Brazil**

This book deals with two very large and often amorphous concepts: *privacy* and *surveillance* in the contexts of government and the marketplace.

Both concepts have undergone changes over the millennia of recorded human history, and those changes have dramatically sped up and expanded over the past few centuries, starting with the widespread use of the printing press in the mid- to late-15th century, when books and newspapers began to proliferate across Europe, and in the rest of the "civilized" world by the end of the 17th century.

The development of radio, television, and the internet in the 20th century heightened the need to define more clearly what both concepts meant and how they applied both to governments (the *public sector*) and to individual and corporate players (the *private sector*).

The Thought Police and Big Brother are terms introduced into the popular lexicon by George Orwell in his novel *1984;*

Big Brother was the overweening, all-powerful government of Orwell's novel, and the Thought Police were those who managed to burrow so deeply into every citizen's behavior, speech, and even thoughts that they could control or punish behavior based on the slightest deviations from orthodoxy.

Orwell was only slightly off the mark. Big Brother types of government, and Thought Police types of social control, are now widespread in the world and incompatible with democracy, as I'll show in more detail later in the book.

Most concerning for Americans and citizens of other "democratic" nations, the mentality of both has heavily infiltrated both American government and corporate sectors, reaching so deeply into the day-to-day details of our lives that the techniques and technologies they use can—and do—not only control but *predict* our behavior.

The goal of those who violate privacy and use surveillance is almost always social control and behavior modification. Setting aside pure voyeurism, those are the areas where money is made, power is accumulated, and political or business goals are reached.

And whether they are of government or of corporate Big Brother, the goals are largely the same and consistent with those just mentioned.

Secrets are now for government and giant corporations to know and hold, but not for average people. And they're used by Big Brother to both acquire and hold power.

J. Edgar Hoover had secrets to hide, for example, so he knew well their power. A gay man at the pinnacle of American power, for most of his life the FBI director knew that in many

US states he and his lover, Clyde Tolson, could be prosecuted and sent to prison for their private, consensual behavior.

Yet Hoover and Tolson lived together, and their relationship was an open secret among Washington's cognoscenti. I still remember a beautiful summer day in Ireland, Louise and I sitting in the living room of author Anthony Summers and his wife, Robbyn, as they described to us the shocking details of Hoover's life and abuses of power they'd uncovered writing *Official and Confidential: The Secret Life of J. Edgar Hoover*.[1]

That books like Summers's weren't published until after Hoover's death is a striking testimonial to the power of surveillance and the blackmail material it can produce to keep powerful people's secrets hidden even from the world's best investigative journalists. Every politician or reporter of any consequence knew that Hoover had a file on him (they were almost all men back then, and powerful men at that time were far more likely to harbor salacious secrets), ensuring Hoover an unbroken hold over the FBI from its founding in 1935 to his 1977 death.

But Hoover didn't use his massive FBI surveillance powers just to cow politicians and reporters; he also was interested in advancing policies close to his heart. A dedicated white supremacist running an FBI where all meaningful power was held in white hands throughout his life,[2] Hoover (or an underling at his behest) famously sent FBI surveillance tapes of Dr. Martin Luther King Jr. having an extramarital affair to the civil rights leader himself, implying that they'd next go to his wife and the public if he didn't commit suicide.[3]

Hoover also spent his entire career downplaying the role of Italian organized crime in the United States, because, among other things, Mafia godfather Santo Trafficante had the goods on his sexual orientation and regularly hosted him and Tolson for gambling junkets.

When, in 1961, Attorney General Robert F. Kennedy over-ruled Hoover and began prosecuting the mob, with the number of cases brought shooting up from dozens annually to over 700 a year in the early 1960s, the Mafia backlash eventually destroyed the Kennedy dynasty.[4]

There's a more modern story of how surveillance and invasions of privacy have impacted American politics: the rise to the presidency of serial rapist, wannabe fascist, and crooked businessman Donald Trump.

The biggest Big Brother of the corporate world, Facebook, had for years been compiling massive troves of personal data on Americans (even Americans without a Facebook account, as any page with a Facebook Like logo on it can send your browsing activity back to Facebook), and sometime in the mid-2010s Cambridge Analytica hired a data scientist to put together an app that could suck down that data without Facebook's knowledge.

Cambridge once bragged that they ended up with more than 4,000 data points on each of 230 million Americans from that effort,[5] but Facebook founder and CEO Mark Zuckerberg identified the number as probably being 87 million Americans.[6]

This information was used by the Donald Trump 2016 and Ted Cruz 2018 campaigns to micro-target Facebook users for highly specific advertisements that essentially weaponized their own private lives to influence them to vote for Trump or to not bother voting for Hillary Clinton.

Brittany Kaiser is the former director of business development at Cambridge Analytica, a subject of the Netflix Original documentary *The Great Hack*, and author of *Targeted: The Cambridge Analytica Whistleblower's Inside Story of How Big Data, Trump, and Facebook Broke Democracy and How It Can Happen Again*.

In a 2019 article for *Fast Company* titled "If Trump Wins in 2020, Blame Facebook," she wrote, "My former colleagues ran data-driven social media targeting programs for both the Trump campaign and a pro-Trump superPAC backed by the Mercer family, also known as the 'Defeat Crooked Hillary' campaign."

Campaigns like that, she alleged, "chose to dance on the line of our legal system, pushing the boundaries of hate speech and disinformation that would normally be considered illegal. Incitement of racial hatred, for example, would land most normal people in jail, but is allowed to proliferate on Facebook and other social media platforms paid for by politicians and their supporters."

The Trump campaign, which she wrote spent "over $100 million promoting lies about Hillary and suppressing Democratic turnout," used "deterrence" as their key word to describe "voter suppression." The goal was to identify probable Democratic voters with a "weak" preference for Clinton and to then persuade them to not bother going to the polls.

Kaiser added, "They promoted fear-based falsehoods demeaning women, Mexicans, and African Americans. Seeing the internal case studies after the election shook me to my core."

She noted, "In traditional politics, voter suppression was more obvious: putting polling booths in far away places, allowing endless lines to convince would-be voters to give up, or even enforcing last-minute requirements of new identification for voter registration. Today, voter suppression takes place digitally, so you can't see it and call it out for what it is."[7]

For example, wrote Issie Lapowsky for *Wired* magazine, "[o]n any given day . . . the [Trump] campaign was running 40,000 to 50,000 variants of its ads, testing how they performed in different formats, with subtitles and without, and static versus video, among other small differences. On the day of the third presidential debate in October, the team ran 175,000 variations."[8]

Thousands of subtle points were used that may have influenced a particular type of person, whether they owned a particular type of bicycle or motorcycle, liked to wear a particular brand of jeans, had relatives who were gay or of a different race, or may have visited a porn or study-prep site (all hypothetical data points, as the true details are still entirely secret), to not bother to vote for Hillary Clinton in 2016. Every day the fine-tuning became more and more precise.

And almost none of the ads were ever shown to the general public or found by journalists. A report in the *Washington Post* noted that "[m]ore than half of the voters the database marked for 'Deterrence' messages were Black, Asian or Latino, with particularly high percentages in predominantly Black neighborhoods in key areas such as Pennsylvania, Wisconsin and Florida."[9]

The result was a direct assault on democracy—just what the Trump campaign had hoped for.

As Sabrina Tavernise wrote of the election results in Wisconsin for the *New York Times* a few weeks after the election,

[B]y local standards, [Black voter turnout] was a disappointment, the lowest turnout in 16 years. And those no-shows were important. Mr. Trump won the state by just 27,000 voters.

Milwaukee's lowest-income neighborhoods offer one explanation for the turnout figures. Of the city's 15 council districts, the decline in turnout from 2012 to 2016 in the five poorest was consistently much greater than the drop seen in more prosperous areas—accounting for half of the overall decline in turnout citywide.

The biggest drop was here in District 15, a stretch of fading wooden homes, sandwich shops and fast-food restaurants that is 84 percent black. In this district, voter turnout declined by 19.5 percent from 2012 figures, according to Neil Albrecht, executive director of the City of Milwaukee Election Commission.[10]

An article for the Madison, Wisconsin, *Capitol Times* stated that Trump carried Wisconsin by a mere 27,000 votes, in part because "[t]urnout was down in most counties throughout the state, but particularly in Milwaukee County, where nearly 60,000 fewer votes were cast this year than in 2012. Clinton earned about 43,000 fewer votes in the Democratic stronghold than Barack Obama did four years ago."[11]

If Trump's ads targeting minorities had run on TV or in the newspapers, everybody would have known what they said, and the Clinton campaign could have rebutted them. But because the only people who saw them were those targeted, and within a day or so they vanished from Facebook (one writer has found 5,000 "receipts" but still no actual ads), it's impossible to know how consequential they were.

Many politicians simply believed Clinton ran a flawed campaign; immediately after the election, I was quick to blame her and campaign manager Robby Mook for the loss. But then I knew nothing about how Trump's campaign used Big Brother strategies via Cambridge Analytica and Facebook.

Neither did I know then what Andrew "Boz" Bosworth, described by the *New York Times* as a "longtime Facebook executive and confidant of Mark Zuckerberg," would write in a 2020 memo to company insiders. Boz, who was in charge of Facebook's advertising from 2015 through 2020, wrote, "So was Facebook responsible for Donald Trump getting elected? I think the answer is yes."

He argued that Trump won because of the "single best digital ad campaign I've ever seen from any advertiser," although he also pointed out that Russian trolls had used the platform to polarize American voters. "[T]he Russians worked to exploit existing divisions in the American public for example by hosting Black Lives Matter and Blue Lives Matter protest events in the same city on the same day," Boz wrote. "The people who [showed] up to those events were real even if the event coordinator was not."[12]

Secrecy and anonymous communication have always been tools of politics.

When the Founders of America conspired to raise a rebellion against the British, they used secrecy and exploited Britain's Castle Doctrine privacy laws to keep their insurrection undercover. They met in secret, and people who operated in secret posted pamphlets and flyers on trees and buildings.

The flyers that kicked off the Boston Tea Party in 1773, which turned most of the Founders from advocates for working with Britain into revolutionary insurgents, included one from an enigmatic Rusticus that proclaimed the following:

Are we in like Manner to be given up to the Disposal of the East India Company, who have now the Assurance, to step forth in Aid of the Minister, to execute his Plan, of enslaving America? . . .

Fifteen hundred Thousands, it is said, perished by Famine in one Year, not because the Earth denied its Fruits; but [because] this Company and their Servants engulfed all the Necessaries of Life, and set them at so high a Rate that the poor could not purchase them.[13]

Such language would have gotten whoever was using the pen name Rusticus imprisoned or perhaps even executed, but they could pull it off by operating in secret.

However, even then, the statements were largely public. Every iteration of politics in America from 1776 to 2015 operated along similar lines. One person could talk with a single other person or a small group in secret; one person could talk to many people in secret by anonymously posting pamphlets.

But that was it.

Until Trump and Big Brother social media came along.

Now, instead of one person talking with one other person, one person can talk with 100 million people in more than 150,000 different ways instantaneously, making any sort of psychological resistance nearly impossible.

Today, shadowy forces—some clearly aligned with hostile foreign governments—are starting and spreading conspiracy theories and alternative realities through opaque social media. The new beliefs adopted by the targets of these campaigns totally alter American politics with almost no media notice or oversight and little discussion in the public sphere.

This new and profoundly high-impact form of messaging has altered the fate and course of American democracy—as well as that of governments all over the globe.

As Paul Mozur said in a *New York Times* article headlined "A Genocide Incited on Facebook, With Posts From Myanmar's Military": "Members of the Myanmar military were the prime operatives behind a systematic campaign on Facebook that stretched back half a decade and that targeted the country's mostly Muslim Rohingya minority group, the people said. The military exploited Facebook's wide reach in Myanmar, where it is so broadly used that many of the country's 18 million internet users confuse the Silicon Valley social media platform with the internet. Human rights groups blame the anti-Rohingya propaganda for inciting murders, rapes and the largest forced human migration in recent history."[14]

Authoritarian, antidemocratic governments across the world—the worst kinds of Big Brother—are not just monitoring their citizens' social media activity but in many cases doing what the Myanmar military did: inserting their own memes and news to disrupt homegrown resistance and pro-democracy movements. China has gone so far as to create their own social media companies and ecosystems while blocking American and other companies with the "Great Firewall."

Because none of this is done in traditional "billboard" media like radio/TV/magazine/newspaper/online ads but instead is microtargeted on social media and via email, it's functionally invisible. That radically increases the difficulty that a democracy faces when trying to fight back without becoming an autocracy itself.

This constellation of surveillance tools and hypertargeted advertising, along with the emergence of Big Brother in both our economic and political spheres, is insidious because it's hidden in plain sight, but only a few giant corporations actually control it.

When just a handful of people and corporations have access to these surveillance and behavioral modification tools, our democracy erodes because that tiny group of fabulously wealthy people has unmatched power to direct our economy and our government, as well as our society, our norms, and our culture as a whole.

As we will see in part 1 of this book, many of these tools are simply evolutions of early forms of social control and mass behavioral modification.

What we thought was just a sophisticated new way to sell us trinkets and lifestyle products has turned out to be a powerful technique to twist governance itself, bending nations away from the democratic "consent of the governed" to something that resembles 20th-century fascism but is much, much harder to stop.

PART ONE

Big Brother and Social Control

Big Brother and the Puritans

The tale is one of an evil time,
When souls were fettered and thought was crime,
And heresy's whisper above its breath
Meant shameful scouring and bonds and death!

—John Greenleaf Whittier, "How the Women Went from Dover"

Big Brother–style social control—the control of behavior and ultimately even thought and belief—has a history as long as human memory. From *The Epic of Gilgamesh* to the Bible to the early American colonies to today, surveillance and the threat of violence have been its principal instruments.

Benjamin Franklin was one of the most influential of the Founders when it came to the shaping of the Constitution and our nation, and he was horrified by the power that the Puritans had seized in his birth state of Massachusetts and nearby New Hampshire.

As a teenager, he fled the state for Philadelphia, where there were no religious tests and people weren't required by law (as they were in most of Massachusetts and New Hampshire) to tithe and attend church every week.

"Scarcely was I arrived at fifteen years of age," he wrote in his first autobiography, "when, after having doubted in turn of different tenets, according as I found them combated in the different books that I read, I began to doubt of revelation itself."[1]

Franklin knew that Big Brother had been with us since the earliest days of this nation, and even when it's used to enforce morality, it's really about power and political control.

This knowledge led him to campaign against organized religion for much of his life. As his peer Joseph Priestly wrote of him, "It is much to be lamented that a man of Dr. Franklin's general good character and great influence should have been an unbeliever in Christianity and also have done so much as he did to make others unbelievers."[2]

But as much as the Founders and Framers rejected Britain's Big Brother political and economic control, they also listened to Franklin and rejected efforts by various churches to insert Christianity into the Constitution. The reason they were so outspoken was pretty straightforward: they had seen firsthand what a religious Big Brother state looked like in New England.

Louise and I used to live just a short drive from Dover, New Hampshire, the fourth-largest city in the state, near the Maine border and the Atlantic seacoast. Long before slavery was widespread in America, the mainstream churches of the colonies were enforcing social control, and John Greenleaf Whittier's poem "How the Women Went from Dover" tells the tale of three young women who dared to challenge that day's social, political, and religious order.

Whittier's poem begins:

> *The tossing spray of Cocheco's fall*
> *Hardened to ice on its rocky wall,*
> *As through Dover town in the chill, gray dawn,*
> *Three women passed, at the cart-tail drawn!*

The three women were Anne Coleman, Mary Tomkins, and Alice Ambrose, and their crime was adhering to and promoting Quaker beliefs in a Congregationalist town.[3]

This so enraged the minister of Dover's Congregational church, John Reyner, that he and church elder Hatevil Nutter lobbied the crown magistrate, Captain Richard Walderne, to have them punished for their challenge to Reyner's authority.

It was a bitter winter in 1662 when Walderne complied, ordering the three women to be stripped to the waist and tied to the back of a horse-drawn cart by their wrists, then dragged through town while receiving ten lashes each. As Whittier wrote:

> *Bared to the waist, for the north wind's grip*
> *And keener sting of the constable's whip,*
> *The blood that followed each hissing blow*
> *Froze as it sprinkled the winter snow.*

A local man, George Bishop, wrote at the time, "Deputy Waldron caused these women to be stripped naked from the middle upwards, and tied to a cart, and after awhile cruelly whipped them, whilst the priest stood and looked and laughed at it."[4]

It was a start, from Reverend Reyner's point of view, but hardly enough to scare the residents of the entire region from which he drew his congregation. So he got the young women's punishment extended to 11 nearby towns over 80 miles of snow-covered roads, all following the same routine.

> *So into the forest they held their way,*
> *By winding river and frost-rimmed bay,*
> *Over wind-swept hills that felt the beat*
> *Of the winter sea at their icy feet.*

The next town was Hampton, where the constable decided that just baring them above the waist wasn't enough. As Sewell's *The History of the People Called Quakers* records, "So he stripped them, and then stood trembling whip in hand, and so he did the execution. Then he carried them to Salisbury through the dirt and the snow half the leg deep; and here they were whipped again."[5]

> *Once more the torturing whip was swung,*
> *Once more keen lashes the bare flesh stung.*
> *"Oh, spare! they are bleeding!" a little maid cried,*
> *And covered her face the sight to hide.*

Whipping, beating, stoning, hanging, nailing, being pilloried (publicly clamped to a post through neck and wrist holes, often naked and sometimes for days at a time), dragging, burning, branding, and dozens of other techniques were employed by Big Brother religious and government authorities in the early American colonies to enforce thought and behavior.

> *If her cry from the whipping-post and jail*
> *Pierced sharp as the Kenite's driven nail,*
> *O woman, at ease in these happier days,*
> *Forbear to judge of thy sister's ways!*

On July 17, 1658, for example, Massachusetts Puritans seized Quakers Christopher Holder and John Copeland and chopped off each man's right ear. They were then imprisoned and brutally whipped "on a set schedule" for "nine weeks straight."

Expelled from the Massachusetts territory, Holder and Copeland were told that if they returned, their left ears would also be cut off and a hole would be bored through each of their tongues with a hot poker.[6]

In 1850, Nathaniel Hawthorne published *The Scarlet Letter*, set in Puritan Boston, which dramatized how rulebreakers were stigmatized in Massachusetts. In Hawthorne's telling, Hester Prynne was forced to wear a scarlet "A," stigmatizing her as an adulterer.

It's why there was debate about admitting Massachusetts to the new United States if they wouldn't drop their laws supporting religion; the state finally, after massive debate and over the objections of multiple churches, complied and agreed to ratify the Constitution.

In each of these examples and many more, the Puritans were simply enforcing a statewide social order designed to control religious thought and behavior and suppress democracy. It drove Franklin to write, "I have found Christian dogma unintelligible. Early in life, I absented myself from Christian assemblies."[7]

Churches, priests, and pastors were that generation's Big Brother in New England, and it was specifically against their power that young Ben Franklin fled Massachusetts for religiously free Philadelphia. It motivated him to work as hard as he did to get the ban on religious tests for public office, the right to be free of religion, and the right of Americans "to be secure in their persons, houses, papers, and effects" into the body of the Constitution and the First and Fourth Amendments.

Big Brother in the Slave Trade

*Christopher Columbus not only opened the door to a
New World, but also set an example for us all.*

—**George H. W. Bush, 1989 speech**

In George Orwell's *1984*, part of Big Brother's power comes from strict application and enforcement of the doctrine that "Who controls the past control the future. Who controls the present controls the past."

At the time of this writing, a battle is raging across our nation to determine what we teach our children about our past. Conservatives decry critical race theory as an affront to American history, but they're not really fighting against critical race theory—they're fighting for control of the past . . . so they can continue to enforce a white-supremacist future.

Slavery as a form of economic and social control didn't start out as a race-based institution, at least not if race is defined by the color of one's skin.

Author Daniel Quinn hypothesized that slavery was the natural outgrowth of the agricultural revolution 7,000 years ago, because with harvest-season food surpluses and winter and spring food shortages, small numbers of people could seize control of the harvest and "lock up the food."[8]

Food being essential to survival, everybody else had to do whatever the food hoarders demanded, leading to humanity's first "wealthy" people, the first caste system, and eventually to outright slavery.

Agriculture, Quinn hypothesized, was the mother of Big Brother.

Anthropologist Peter Farb, in his brilliant 1968 book *Man's Rise to Civilization as Shown by the Indians of North America from Primeval Times to the Coming of the Industrial State*, lays out the structure of several dozen Native American tribes at the time of first contact with Europeans.[9]

Farb wrote that the only Native American societies that practiced slavery—something extraordinarily rare among American tribes—were those where food was highly seasonal. He profiles, for example, a tribe in the Pacific Northwest whose primary protein source was the annual run of salmon as one of the few that practiced slavery; they also stored enormous amounts of smoked salmon.

From establishing slavery to institutionalizing it, the tribes that held slaves had often different, but in some ways consistent, ways of thinking about and dehumanizing their enslaved people. It's a pattern also repeated in Western history.

Twenty-four hundred years ago, Aristotle, in his book *Politics*, observed, "Seeing then that the state is made up of households, before speaking of the state we must speak of the management of the household," and that "a complete household consists of slaves and freemen."

Noting that household management means having the "proper instruments" for the job, Aristotle said, "Now instruments are of various sorts; some are living, others lifeless. . . . And so, in the arrangement of the family, a slave is a living possession, and property a number of such instruments; and the servant is himself an instrument which takes precedence of all other instruments."[10]

Aristotle's slaves, however, looked pretty much like Aristotle himself. A famous statue of his mentor's mentor Socrates' daughter Mnesarete's death, for example, shows her slave, a young woman indistinguishable from any other Greek of the day.

Slaves in the Greek and Roman empires were drawn from the poor, people convicted of crimes, prisoners of war, and the occasional Persian or European who'd been captured and transported to Athens.

Athens's slave population in the fifth century BCE census was around 80,000 (out of a total population of about 300,000), and all but the poor had multiple slaves, mostly for household work.

Similarly, in the Bible, the Books of Exodus, Leviticus, and Deuteronomy have specific instructions for the treatment of enslaved people. Some were Hebrews, others prisoners of war from nearby tribes. Most probably looked very much like the patriarchs who owned them.

The New Testament includes references to slavery as well. "Let all who are under the yoke of slavery regard their masters as worthy of all honor, so that the name of God and the teaching may not be blasphemed," reads 1 Timothy 6:1. Paul's letter to the Ephesians includes this: "Slaves, obey your earthly masters with fear and trembling, in singleness of heart, as you obey Christ."[11]

Again, though, most of those slaves looked very much like the people enslaving them.

The task of racializing slavery fell to the good men of Virginia, a colony established by the East India Company and the British government in 1607 at Jamestown. (The colony was named after the Virgin Queen, Elizabeth I, and the town was named after the Company's largest stockholder, King James I.)

Tobacco developed as a cash crop in Virginia but was labor-intensive to produce, so the colonists began to import bonded Europeans and Africans around 1620. Both could work off their bonds, typically seven to 15 years, and then would be freed. Europeans, who made up about three-quarters of the bonded servants at that time, typically had shorter times to acquire their freedom, while some Africans were bonded for life with freedom promised only to their children.[12]

But as the number of freed former bondsmen increased over time, so did their discontent with the distribution of wealth and land. This culminated in Bacon's Rebellion, when Nathaniel Bacon led an insurrection of both white and Black freed bondsmen, burning much of Jamestown to the ground in 1676.

The outgrowth of this era was the realization that time-limited bonds were nowhere as efficient as total outright chattel slavery, where the enslaved people were the *permanent* property of their owner and could even be passed down to future generations of slave owners.

Many of the European bonded men were drawn from the lower classes of the Germans, Irish and Scots, regarded at the time by those of English ancestry as "inferior races," as Noel Ignatiev documents in detail in his book *How the Irish Became White*.[13]

After a decade in the colonies, many of these people could dress and talk with an accent like the colonists themselves, so defining bonded or freeman status purely by skin color became an easy solution to the confusion emerging in the mid-17th century.

But that didn't solve the problem of formerly bonded free white men, particularly those who weren't of British (Anglo-

Saxon) ancestry, who were still seething with the rage that fueled Bacon's Rebellion. To bring them into the fold, the colonists of Virginia needed an entirely new American Big Brother invention: whiteness.

Big Brother Invents "Whiteness" to Keep Power

Whiteness is primarily defined by what's *denied* to people who are *not* white.

In his book *White by Law*, Ian Lopez refers to whiteness as "a double negative": its power comes from racializing *everybody else* who's nonwhite, while it doesn't touch or affect white people themselves, who are "not non-White."[14] That's why most white people are unaware of the dimensions and privileges of their own whiteness; they don't experience the privations that come along with being not-white.

Whiteness requires not that whites acknowledge what they have (they're rarely aware of that), but instead that they allow, mostly by ignoring its structure, a society to exist where nonwhite people are separated from and denied the fruits of being white.

Whiteness means having it all, or at least the *opportunity* to have it all. Within that frame, advocates for the perpetuation of whiteness have built entire edifices of self-help and an elaborate "pull yourself up by your bootstraps" mythology.

I've done very well in life, having started a half-dozen businesses and grown several of them to multimillion-dollar status before selling each to retire for a few years with my wife and kids. I have success, a reasonable savings, and a nice house. But if I'd been Black when I was born in 1951, it would have been a very, very different story.

Growing up, my own whiteness was invisible to me until my later adult years. When conservatives railed about "personal responsibility" and how "lazy" Black people and other minorities were, my education and acculturation hadn't provided me with any sort of an informational or historical frame to rebut them.

It was my whiteness that helped me, as scholar Peggy McIntosh wrote, through "an invisible weightless knapsack of special provisions, maps, passports, codebooks, visas, clothes, tools, and blank checks."[15]

Little did I realize that my whiteness—as a legal and social construct—was largely an American invention. The good Fathers of Virginia brought us this reality in the mid-1600s by changing the bond and debt laws.

At that time, much of the labor in the American colonies, from farm and factory work to rustling cattle and building houses, was done by people compelled to work for free for a certain number of years.

Sometimes that "bond"—the years of work owed as a debt—was in exchange for sea passage from Europe to North America; other times it was a way for European prisoners to get a "new start" in the New World (and those bonds were sometimes for the person's entire life). In every case, bonded laborers from Europe were indentured to their masters for a specific number of years.

Virginia's creation of modern-day whiteness started with a 1660 law that reserved bond terms shorter than life exclusively to people who'd come from "Christian nations," thus excluding all the Africans who'd been brought against their will to Virginia. At that time, Virginia had about 24,000 bonded European laborers and 6,000 from Africa.

Around 1670, Virginia passed a law stating that any non-Christian bonded laborers brought to the colony by sea must serve their entire lives. In 1680, they made law that explicitly named all persons from Africa as slaves for life. As a result, the flow of bonded Europeans was reduced to a trickle (but was still coming full-on into New England and Northern states in that region); virtually all bonded laborers arriving in Virginia were now Africans.

Other Southern states followed Virginia's lead within a decade as England, in the late 1600s, jumped into the slave trade with both feet.

Virginia still had quite a few Black laborers who'd served out their bonds and were legally free men and women, so the Virginia legislature began making it harder and harder for them to enjoy any sort of a normal life in the colony.

While the English law that the colonies operated under specified that the bond status of a father determined the status of his child, as more and more Virginia farm, factory, and plantation owners fathered "mulatto" children by raping enslaved African women, in 1662 Virginia changed the law to specify the mother's status as defining that of her child.

In 1664, they passed a law specifying that any free woman of any race who married a bonded man would immediately be reduced to the bond status of her new husband; the law was designed to discourage interracial marriage, which, while rare, was a growing phenomenon.

In 1691, the Virginia legislature passed a law for the "prevention of that abominable mixture and spurious issue" caused by the intermarriage of men of color (including Native Americans) with "English or other white women."[16]

Throughout this time, the word "white" was increasingly replacing "Christian," "free," and even "bonded" in legal descriptions of European-descended persons: whiteness was becoming a thing, as the Big Brother of Virginia's government used it more and more aggressively to maintain social control and to build the wealth of the white plantation-owner class, the oligarchs of the day, now that enslaved Black persons were purely property and could be bought, sold, or passed down through generations.

Bacon's Rebellion, in which free but poor whites fought on the same side as poor free Africans, taught Virginia's power brokers a lesson: legally separate the races in every way possible, and grant special privileges to poor whites to break their sense of solidarity with poor but free people of other races, particularly Africans.

To amplify this notion, Virginia tightened the screws on free Blacks, mulattoes, and Native Americans.

In 1670, freed Blacks were banned from importing their own bonded labor to work their farms; the Virginia legislature passed a law that year barring them not just from importing but even from purchasing laborers of any sort. It began the ruination of nonwhite farming and other operations.

In 1705, Virginia passed a law that allowed bonded Europeans to own livestock but stipulated that any livestock owned by bonded Africans could be confiscated by local authorities and given to poor but free whites anytime they pleased.

Free Blacks were still voting in Virginia until 1723, although they couldn't hold public office or bear witness in a criminal or civil trial against a white person; that year, Virginia outlawed voting by *any* person of even partial African ancestry under *any* circumstances.

By the following decade, when most of the Virginians among the Founding generation were born, whiteness had acquired a specific legal and social meaning, by defining fences around the behaviors of everybody who wasn't white.

The double negative had so transformed American politics and society that by the time of the Declaration of Independence in 1776, the enslavement of people of even partial African, Asian, or Native American ancestry was legal in all 13 states: whiteness was now defined by how law (replacing social norms) restricted people who were not-white.[17]

The old distinctions of the "Celtic race" or the "Teutonic race" were largely washed away as those people who were not Black or brown or red were newly classified as "white." As law and social construct, whiteness was now a thing.

By the 1800s, as new states joined the union, each did away with any restrictions (such as requiring property ownership or being free of debt) on men voting, but they explicitly added the word *white* as a restriction to voting and many other forms of civic participation to their new constitutions and laws. This happened in Ohio in 1803, Indiana in 1816, Illinois in 1818, Michigan in 1837, Iowa in 1846, Wisconsin in 1848, California in 1850, and Oregon in 1859.[18]

Frederick Douglass: Mental Emancipation Leads to Social Emancipation

In the first book in this series, *The Hidden History of Guns and the Second Amendment*, I wrote at length about how the Second Amendment was written the way it was, at the time it was, to ensure the survival of the slave patrols in several Southern states.

But guns weren't the primary instrument of Big Brother's social control in the pre–Civil War era: literacy was.

In 1818, when Frederick Augustus Washington Bailey was born to an enslaved Black mother in Maryland, the main instrument of social control of Black bodies was called the "pass system."

All the way back to the 1600s, white owners of enslaved Black people would write "passes" so their slaves could travel outside the farm, factory, or plantation to pick up supplies, deliver crops or other goods, and fulfill other justified purposes.

There was little standardization of these passes until the early 1800s; most were simply a scrap or piece of paper saying that the person who carried it—usually named, and sometimes identified by height, weight, or other descriptive marks—could travel.

Bailey, who later took the name Douglass after he escaped slavery, recalled in his autobiography when and how he realized that he could use the pass system to escape the enslavement into which he was born.

"The frequent hearing of my mistress reading the Bible aloud," Douglass wrote, "for she often read aloud when her husband was absent, awakened my curiosity in respect to this *mystery* of reading, and roused in me the desire to learn. Up to this time I had known nothing whatever of this wonderful art, and my ignorance and inexperience of what it could do for me, as well as my confidence in my mistress, emboldened me to ask her to teach me to read."

Mrs. Hugh Auld apparently didn't know that by that time, Maryland, like several other slave states, had outlawed teaching reading and writing to enslaved Black people.

"With an unconsciousness and inexperience equal to my own," Douglass wrote, "she readily consented, and in an incredibly short time, by her kind assistance, I had mastered the alphabet and could spell words of three or four letters. My mistress seemed almost as proud of my progress as if I had been her own child, and supposing that her husband would be as well pleased, she made no secret of what she was doing for me."

This was when young Frederick Douglass learned that reading was forbidden to him and people like him.

Indeed, she exultingly told him of the aptness of her pupil and of her intention to persevere, as she felt it her duty to do, in teaching me, at least, to read the Bible. And here arose the first dark cloud over my Baltimore prospects, the precursor of chilling blasts and drenching storms. Master Hugh was astounded beyond measure and, probably for the first time, proceeded to unfold to his wife the true philosophy of the slave system, and the peculiar rules necessary in the nature of the case to be observed in the management of human chattels. Of course he forbade her to give me any

*further instruction, telling her in the first place that to do so
was unlawful, as it was also unsafe; "for," said he, "if you
give a nigger an inch he will take an ell. Learning will spoil
the best nigger in the world. If he learns to read the Bible it
will forever unfit him to be a slave. He should know nothing
but the will of his master, and learn to obey it. . . . If you
teach him how to read, he'll want to know how to write,
and this accomplished, he'll be running away with himself."*

The realization was both enlightening and horrifying to
young Frederick:

*The effect of his words on me was neither slight nor transi-
tory. His iron sentences, cold and harsh, sunk like heavy
weights deep into my heart, and stirred up within me a
rebellion not soon to be allayed.*

*This was a new and special revelation, dispelling a pain-
ful mystery against which my youthful understanding had
struggled, and struggled in vain, to wit, the white man's
power to perpetuate the enslavement of the black man.
"Very well," thought I. "Knowledge unfits a child to be a
slave." I instinctively assented to the proposition, and from
that moment I understood the direct pathway from slavery
to freedom.*[19]

Douglass used his newfound literacy to escape slavery in
1838, using "protection papers" he could read that were given
him by a formerly enslaved but then-free African American
seaman. The seaman's wife gave young Douglass a sailor's uni-
form to enhance the ruse.

Literacy, a direct violation of the thought police of Virginia's
Big Brother police state, emancipated Douglass's mind, which

in turn allowed him to help push our entire country toward an entirely new future of social emancipation.

He went on to become one of America's most eloquent public speakers, statesmen, and well-known authors, and his career and writing fostered a movement for civil rights and true democracy that endures to this day.

It's hard to imagine that Frederick Douglass could have become literate if his slave owners had the Big Brother surveillance tools available in our society today. It's likewise hard to imagine that the civil rights and pro-democracy movements (or any social movement) could have endured if individuals did not have a right to privacy.

Why the Founders Didn't Explicitly Protect Our Privacy

At the founding of our republic, the concept of privacy was well known, but the word *privacy* was rarely used to describe it.

The Fourth Amendment, for example, says clearly, "The right of the people to be secure in their persons, houses, papers, and effects, against unreasonable searches and seizures, shall not be violated," but never references "privacy."[20]

In all of the founding documents, in fact, from the Declaration of Independence to the Federalist Papers to the US Constitution, the word *privacy* appears only once, and that's in a context that most of us would never use to describe privacy today.

Indeed, with a digital search of every word written by the Declaration's author, Thomas Jefferson (which fills 20 volumes in print), and every word spoken at the Constitutional

Convention and recorded by "Father of the Constitution" James Madison, you'll not find even one single instance of the word *privacy*.

The one lonely example from a Founder comes from a newspaper article published in 1788 to promote ratification of the Constitution. "If we compare the publicity which must necessarily attend the mode of appointment by the President and an entire branch of the national legislature," Alexander Hamilton wrote in *Federalist*, no. 69, "with the *privacy* in the mode of appointment by the governor of New York, *closeted in a secret apartment* with at most four, and frequently with only two persons . . . we cannot hesitate to pronounce that the power of the chief magistrate of this State, in the disposition of offices, must, in practice, be greatly superior to that of the Chief Magistrate of the Union [emphasis mine]."[21]

What Hamilton was saying here has nothing to do with privacy as we understand it today. He was pointing out that when a person is appointed by a small number of people in secret, it actually gives him or her more latitude to act without a threat of losing that power than when a larger number of people, like the entire nation selecting a president, vote for a leader.

The reason is simple: the president is answerable to a much larger populace than the governor of New York, who in that day was answerable to only a handful of individuals, who literally operated in secret and were usually his personal friends.

This single use of the word *privacy* in all of our consequential founding documents by Hamilton shows how the word was really understood at that time: it referred to things done in secret.

Thus, the main reason the word *privacy* rarely occurs in the founding documents of this country is that it had a quite different meaning at the time from today's understanding of the word. More often than not, in fact, *privacy* referred to something everybody did every day but always tried to do in secret: using what we today call the toilet.

Most people of a certain age or who've lived in a rural setting know that outhouses are often referred to as "privies." This dates back hundreds of years, through and before the Founding era, when people would stand up and move to leave a house to relieve themselves in the outhouse while saying to everybody, "Excuse me, I need a moment of privacy."

Everybody understood that "I want privacy" meant "I need to use the privy." We didn't even start referring to privies as bathrooms until the widespread use of indoor plumbing in the late 19th and early 20th centuries, when bathtubs were first incorporated into the same room as the flush toilet, which was popularized by Thomas Crapper in the 1860s.[22]

This is why outhouses were called *privies*, and it also explains why the Founders of our republic and Framers of the Constitution chose not to use the word *privacy* to describe our right to freedom from government intrusion into our private affairs. It would hardly be decorous to reference toilet functions in a document as grave and solemn as the Constitution, even though the Fourth Amendment clearly speaks of what today we understand to be a major piece of our rights of privacy.

As our use of the word *privacy* and our understanding of the concept evolved throughout the 19th and 20th centuries, it took quite a while for American law to catch up. Privacy, using that word, didn't exist as a constitutional doctrine at law in the United States until 1965, even though without privacy as we understand it today, the American Revolution could never have happened.

In 1961, the United States Supreme Court specifically struck down a right to privacy in the case of *Poe v. Ullman*.[23] That case challenged a Connecticut law that said both unmarried and married couples committed a crime if they were in possession of birth control, and the Court allowed the law to stand.

Justice John Marshall Harlan II issued a scathing dissent in *Poe v. Ullman*, echoing a 1928 dissent by Justice Louis Brandeis in *Olmstead v. United States*.[24] Justice Brandeis, in addition to arguing that there should be a constitutional amendment guaranteeing a specific right to privacy, wrote in his dissent in *Olmstead v. United States* that the Founders "conferred, as against the Government, the right to be let alone—the most comprehensive of rights, and the right most valued by civilized men."[25]

This 1928 screed by Brandeis on what he called the "right to be let alone" shook the legal world, stirring legal and public debate over the right to privacy that lasted more than two generations.

Finally, four years after Justice Harlan's dissent in *Poe*, the Supreme Court reversed that same Connecticut law in *Griswold v. Connecticut* (1965), specifically referencing a "freedom to associate and privacy in one's associations."[26]

The majority of justices on the Court were finally convinced, and Justice William O. Douglas wrote in the decision,

> *The foregoing cases suggest that specific guarantees in the Bill of Rights have penumbras, formed by emanations from those*

guarantees that help give them life and substance. . . . Various guarantees create "zones of privacy." The right of association contained in the penumbra of the First Amendment is one, as we have seen. The Third Amendment, in its prohibition against the quartering of soldiers "in any house" in time of peace without the consent of the owner, is another facet of that privacy. The Fourth Amendment explicitly affirms the "right of the people to be secure in their persons, houses, papers, and effects, against unreasonable searches and seizures." The Fifth Amendment, in its Self-Incrimination Clause, enables the citizen to create a zone of privacy which government may not force him to surrender to his detriment.

Douglas then cited the Ninth Amendment, which says that even though specific rights are laid out in the Constitution, those "shall not be construed to deny or disparage others retained by the people."[27]

While this decision represented a large step toward more widespread use of birth control, which helped invigorate the then-growing women's rights movement and became the foundation for the 1973 *Roe v. Wade* decision, it was also a primary landmark in the modern-day recognition of a right to privacy, a right to defy the patriarchal Big Brothers of the day.

Privacy Evolves in US Law

Two years after the Supreme Court's landmark ruling in *Griswold v. Connecticut*, the Court overruled its own 1928 *Olmstead* decision in *Katz v. United States* (1967) and ruled that wiretapped phone conversations cannot be used as evidence in court *unless they were obtained with a warrant.* In that same ruling, they also explicitly extended Fourth Amendment protections to everywhere a person may have a "reasonable expectation of privacy."[28]

In short order, Congress got into the act.

The Fair Credit Reporting Act of 1970 guaranteed the privacy of an individual's financial data held in corporate hands.[29]

The Privacy Act of 1974 amended Title 5 of the Federal Code to establish clear privacy rights with regard to the collection, maintenance, use, and dissemination of any personal information held by the federal government. It also gives citizens a right to see whatever records the government may be holding on them.[30]

In 1998, the Federal Trade Commission (FTC) implemented the Children's Online Privacy Protection Rule (COPPA), providing parents with weak but real powers over what their children are exposed to on the internet;[31] and the following year, Congress passed the Financial Modernization Act of 1999, which required banks and other financial institutions to disclose to their customers what kinds of personal information they were collecting and how they used it.[32]

On June 6 and 7, 2013, Edward Snowden revealed, in stories written by Glenn Greenwald and published in *The Guardian*, that the National Security Agency (NSA) was using secret—and illegal—court orders to force phone companies and internet service providers (ISPs), respectively, to disclose records on the communications of tens of millions of Americans without their knowledge or consent.[33,34]

The Snowden stories not only set off an explosive public relations disaster for American intelligence agencies and the private, for-profit corporations they'd contracted with (such as the one for which Snowden worked) but also provoked Congress to action.

In 2015, Congress passed the USA Freedom Act, which explicitly banned such bulk data collections, although numerous executive orders (some apparently still secret) and practices within the intelligence community appear to have diluted or entirely gotten around its provisions.[35]

The United States has still gone nowhere near as far as the European Union and several of its individual member states in guaranteeing individual privacy, particularly on the internet, and since 2015 the debate has largely stalled out in the face of billion-dollar lobbying efforts from both social media companies and private, for-profit contractors working for American intelligence agencies.

Another reason Europe may be ahead of us in this regard is that many people in Europe have firsthand experience with life under all-knowing and all-spying Big Brother governments (regardless of ideology), from fascist Italy to Nazi Germany to the former Soviet Union and East Germany.

Surveillance and Social Control in East Germany

In the winter of late 1987, my eldest daughter (then 15) and I left Louise and our younger two kids at a hotel in West Berlin and took the underground train to the area known as Checkpoint Charlie, where we could travel into East Berlin, the capital of East Germany.

We'd lived in West Germany for a bit more than half a year at that point, spending some of our time in a home in Höchheim, literally on the border with East Germany. A few dozen feet from our residence was a dirt road that stretched miles in both directions. On our side of the road was the town of Höchheim and the rolling hills of rural West Germany, covered in snow that time of year but ablaze with flowers and rich with crops during the summer.

On the other side of the road, just six feet off the roadway, was a chain-link fence that seemed at least 20 feet tall, topped with razor wire, extending off toward the horizon in both directions. Forty or so feet deeper into East Germany was a second, identical fence; between the two was a stretch of sand, and both sides were seeded with landmines that had the obnoxious habit of exploding on warm mornings when the snow melted and the ground heaved.

A few hundred feet back from the second fence, deeper inside East Germany, was a rebar-reinforced concrete tower jutting a hundred or more feet into the air like an airport control tower. It was flared out at the top to support the pod where men with binoculars, machine guns, and rifles tracked our every move, often conspicuously pointing their sniper rifles at us when we walked along the border dirt road.

A quarter mile behind them, across a field that was farmed in the summer, was the sister city to Höchheim, Mendhausen. All night, every night, the town was flooded with light; since it was a border town, every house had white-hot floodlights mounted just below the rooflines, pointing out into the yards and streets, and nobody could go outside after sundown.

So we had some small sense of what East Germany must be like.

When we emerged from East German security and climbed the long subway stairs up to the street, there was a short line— perhaps five or six men—waiting at the cabstand next to the station. We never saw a cab, but every 10 or 15 minutes a car would pull up and the driver would have a brief conversation with the first person in line, who'd then jump into the front passenger seat and the car would take off.

After we'd stood in the light snow and freezing wind for an hour or so, a beat-up old black Russian Lata pulled up, and the driver, a young man in his 20s, rolled down his window.

"Need a ride?" he said.

"Are there no cabs?" I said, worried about breaking the law in a foreign country.

"You could wait all day," he said. "They're all having coffee. You're paid here in East Germany whether you work or not, so it's up to us entrepreneurs to keep things going."

"Can you just give us a tour of East Berlin and bring us back here in four or five hours?" I asked. "And what would it cost?"

He quoted me a price that, as I recall, was around US $20 (it was all deutsche marks back then). When we got into his car, me in the front and my daughter in the back, he introduced himself as Toasten, although I later learned that word means "toast" in German, and nobody I knew back in West Germany had ever heard of it as a first name.

Toasten, though, had to know all about us. He said it was so he wouldn't go to jail for running an illegal taxi if we were stopped by the police; we had to become his long-lost cousin and niece from America, he said, so we needed a cover story and he had to know all about our family and past so our stories would line up.

We merrily chatted about the schools I'd attended, the jobs I'd had, where I'd lived and traveled around the world, and my daughter's thoughts on going to gymnasium (high school) in West Germany and what subjects she learned. His English was modest, like my German, so our conversation alternated between the two languages as we filled in words missing from our vocabularies.

The day was otherwise unremarkable: we waited almost an hour in a restaurant for a waiter to pay attention to us (they were all in the corner smoking cigarettes and drinking coffee; Toasten said they got paid whether they served us or not, and tips were not allowed—a theme he repeated frequently) and traveled around a very gray, dreary, and still-war-pocked city lacking even a single sign identifying a store or restaurant.

When we returned, my friends in West Germany joked that I was now in the East German police's files, but it wasn't until 2006, back in the United States, that I realized what had actually happened that winter day. Louise and I watched a German movie, subtitled in English, *The Lives of Others*, about the notorious East German Ministerium für Staatssicherheit (State Security), or, as everybody called them, the Stasi. (It's truly one of the best movies I've ever seen.)[36]

This well-known secret police organization, by the 1980s when I was visiting, had gotten around a third of all six million East Germans to spy on the other two-thirds, through a network of 100,000 employees and two million *inoffizielle Mitarbeiter*, the unofficial collaborators.

Many, if not most, of the collaborators spied on their neighbors because they, themselves, wanted better jobs or living arrangements, which the Stasi could arrange, or were being blackmailed by the Stasi, which maintained meticulous dossiers on every East German and every person who visited the country.[37]

Toasten, on reflection, was either Stasi or reporting to the Stasi. As were the friends, neighbors, relatives, and coworkers of just about every single East German—including those working for or with the Stasi.

In East Germany, from February 1950 until February 1990, neighbors kept track of neighbors and reported their activities and conversations regularly, often being provided with wiretapping equipment so they could listen in to others' living rooms and bedrooms; the police themselves listened to all the phones and monitored faxes.

The storekeepers where people shopped and the service-people who came to fix appliances all reported everything they saw and heard. Pretty much everybody was spying, in one way or another, on pretty much everybody else.

Spying, it could be said, was the principal business of the East German state. They were *almost* as comprehensive in their knowledge of every East German citizen as Facebook, Google, and Amazon are about you and me right now.

That knowledge gave East German Stasi officers and people who worked with them, like Vladimir Putin, the power to threaten, blackmail, or intimidate would-be rebels and to softly discourage everybody else from even thinking of rebellion or engaging with anybody else entertaining such ideas.

We've seen the same Big Brother tools used during the past in this country, from the Puritans to slavery to J. Edgar Hoover's FBI. This is because there are only two primary ways for a government to ensure stability: trust or fear. A government is short-lived when it loses or lacks its citizens' trust *unless* it can replace trust with fear.

US Federal and State Big Brothers

Although Edward Snowden's revelations shocked Americans and the rest of the world as to how extensive the US government's surveillance of its citizens had become—and to what extent it had been privatized (Snowden worked for a private contractor)—government agencies from federal to state to local, including police departments, are sucking up massive amounts of data.

For example, US Customs and Border Protection (CBP)—the agency that former President Donald Trump often brought in as, essentially, a private police force, sending their agents into Portland and Seattle and using them in Washington, DC, to attack Black Lives Matter (BLM) protesters—worked out a deal for "vehicle data extraction kits" made by an American company, Berla, purchased from Swedish company MSAB.

Most people don't realize that when they hook up their smartphone to their car to listen to music, make phone calls, or use maps, they're often transferring much of their private life into the car's internal memory—where it stays.

Sam Biddle, reporting for *The Intercept* in May 2021, wrote that MSAB claims their products helped CPB extract from people's cars "recent destinations, favorite locations, call logs, contact lists, SMS messages, emails, pictures, videos, social media feeds, and the navigation history of everywhere the vehicle has been."

Biddle quotes the founder of Berla noting that most people don't realize that when they plug their phone into a car, even a rental or a friend's car or an Uber with a convenient USB port, "it's going to charge your phone, absolutely. And as soon as it powers up, it's going to start sucking all your data down into the car."

Data? Biddle quotes Berla founder Ben LaMere: "We had a Ford Explorer . . . we pulled the system out, and we recovered 70 phones that had been connected to it. All of their call logs, their contacts and their SMS history, as well as their music preferences, songs that were on their device, and some of their Facebook and Twitter things as well. . . . And it's quite comical when you sit back and read some of the text messages."[38]

Even more problematic are devices often generically referred to as stingrays, the name given one of them by one company. They pretend to be cell towers and give you access to the web and to make calls; when your phone is near one, it connects to the stingray, thinking it's a cell tower, and now all the data on and flowing through your phone, from calls to stored files and pictures to emails and text messages, is sucked up.

When I did a TV show in Washington, DC, I'd often walk home passing by the White House. Most days when I did, my phone would get hot and the battery would lose about half its charge within a three-block walk.

When I learned in 2019 that multiple stingray devices had been planted near the White House (reports suggested they were Israel's, but it could have been any country or even our government), it all made sense.[39] And led me to wonder what they got out of Trump's phone after he made such a big deal out of ignoring cell phone security standards.

But it's not just foreign spies using these contraptions: turns out they're popular across government agencies, right down to local police departments. In 2018, the American Civil Liberties Union (ACLU) reported that it had "identified 75 agencies in 27 states and the District of Columbia that own stingrays, but because many agencies continue to shroud their purchase and use of stingrays in secrecy, this map dramatically underrepresents the actual use of stingrays by law enforcement agencies nationwide."[40]

Police departments all over the country are using them to spy on citizens, as are more than a dozen federal agencies, according to the ACLU.

Entire books have been written about government surveillance in the United States, and the minutiae are far too extensive for this discussion, but the bottom line is that without strong court-based legal standards and a high level of transparent oversight by the press, even the US government could become far more systemically a Big Brother that openly defies democratic norms.

Democracy Requires Trust; Authoritarianism Requires Fear

In *The Hidden History of American Oligarchy*, I laid out how animals, from ants and gnats to birds and fish to dogs and humans, are wired for fairness and majority-rule group decision-making, something we generally call *democracy*.

Sometimes it appears seamless, and only in the past few decades have we learned of the existence of this phenomenon in the animal kingdom. Prior to that, generations of scientists had asserted that pretty much every animal species worked the way medieval European kingdoms did, with a dictatorial alpha dog and a submissive pack. Now we know that's almost never true in nature.

When birds migrate or fish swim in schools, each wingbeat and tail twitch is, essentially, a vote, and the votes of all the members within sight are continuously and instantly tabulated moment-to-moment. Thus, when more than half the birds or fish "vote" to move 20 degrees to the right, for example, suddenly the entire flock or school moves, as if choreographed by telepathy.

Bees and ants vote on which scout to follow to which new food source or new home, and across the range of ruminant mammals from wildebeests to red deer to horses and zebras, when more than 50 percent of the animals point their bodies toward a particular water hole or other place, the entire herd will move. Hyenas even vote by sneezing!

Democracy and fairness are deeply embedded in the history of the human race as well. Cultural anthropologists specializing in tribal people still living as hunter-gatherers—the way the human race appears to have lived for around 300,000 years before the agricultural revolution—point out that virtually all tribal societies are both highly egalitarian and highly democratic.

Benjamin Franklin went out of his way to point this out to his colleagues at the Albany Plan of Union in 1754 when he invited Iroquois elders to open and bless the first day of deliberations.

He later wrote to a friend, "It would be a very strange Thing, if six Nations of Ignorant Savages should be capable of forming a Scheme for such an Union, and be able to execute it in such a Manner, as that it has subsisted Ages, and appears indissoluble; and yet that a like Union should be impracticable for ten or a Dozen English Colonies."[41]

But the history of humanity, particularly since the agricultural revolution, has also been one of Big Brother's use of brutality, theft, and genocide.

This led to the Enlightenment-era split between Thomas Hobbes, who asserted in *Leviathan* in 1651 that without the iron fist of church or state the lives of humans would be "solitary, poor, nasty, brutish, and short," and Jean-Jacques Rousseau and John Locke, later that century, who believed that the inherent nature of humankind was good, and therefore self-governance was not only possible but optimal.

Fortunately, the Founders and Framers were more fans of Locke and Rousseau than of Hobbes. As a result, our democracy is closing in on a quarter of a millennium.

Looking back on that Hobbes/Rousseau split, it's clear that there are two possible currencies that a government can use to hold itself together. They are, as noted earlier, trust and fear.

Governments founded in trust require high levels of transparency and accountability and the regular participation of well over half of their citizens in civic events like voting for representatives. We generally call these *democratic republics*.

Because trust is the currency or power behind these governments, everything from laws and rules to cultural norms promoting mutual trust and participation is necessary. When such governments become opaque and voters don't see their basic needs being met—including their need for privacy—despite regular voting and even protest, such governments are vulnerable to either democratic revolution or antidemocratic takeover.

Anti- and nondemocratic governments don't have trust at their foundation, so they must rely on fear, as did the government of East Germany from 1950 to 1990.

Big Brother–style governments like those of East Germany or today's China or Saudi Arabia actually *want* their citizens to know they're constantly being spied on. Just the *threat* of being caught and punished for antigovernment activities is enough to deter many of them.

Such governments encourage their citizens to pursue more personal or local goals, like climbing the business or social ladder or connecting with sources of entertainment, instead of involving themselves in politics. It's the modern version of the way the later Roman emperors kept people in check as their republic slid into tyranny: *bread and circuses.*

The easiest way any government can persuade its citizenry to forfeit privacy is to convince them that they'll be more *secure* as a result.

This is what Alexis de Tocqueville warned about, and also why the Patriot Act, with its massive erosion of civil liberties, sailed through Congress in the wake of 9/11: Americans were more *afraid* of another concrete terrorist attack than they were of losing their seemingly abstract rights to privacy.

PART TWO

Big Brother and the
Emergence of
Surveillance Capitalism

The Surveillance Industry Is Booming

What is privacy? After all, we can protect something only if we know what it is.

Probably the simplest, universally accepted definition of *privacy* is the idea that your home is your own private domain.

This foundational notion of privacy is a pretty ancient idea.

Sir Edward Coke, in *The Institutes of the Laws of England*, laid it out in 1628: "For a man's house is his castle, *et domus sua cuique est tutissimum refugium* [and each man's home is his safest refuge]."[1] In that, he was citing a law ratified in 1275 by England's King Edward III.[2]

This idea goes *way* back.

So why, when you buy a thermostat to keep the temperature of your home steady, or one that's programmable to cool down at night and warm up during the day, do all of the large vendors of such products require you to let them spy on you?

A "smart" thermostat doesn't just regulate the temperature of your home. As part of the "Internet of Things," it tells the company that sold it to you when you're home and when you're gone, when you sleep and when you're up, and from that data a company can infer a lot of details about your lifestyle and even your medical conditions.

Insomniac? Maybe that bit of data should be added to the thousands of data points used by employers to determine if you'll be a "good" employee.

Keeping the house abnormally warm or cold? Maybe you have cardiovascular disease or are going through menopause, and it's time to raise your insurance rates.

Does the thermostat's motion detector super-frequently notice a person walking by? Maybe you're renting a room to somebody else or you frequently throw parties, indicating that you're a debt or alcoholism risk.

And if a data mining company doesn't want to buy your thermostat's data, the government might.

As CIA director James Clapper told a Senate panel in January 2016, "In the future, intelligence services might use the [Internet of Things] for identification, surveillance, monitoring, location tracking, and targeting for recruitment, or to gain access to networks or user credentials."[3]

And, of course, it's not just your thermostat that's constantly squealing to Big Brother. Your home security system, baby monitor, cell phone, game device, smart TV, fitness watch—even Mattel's talking Barbie doll feeds everything it hears back to the mother ship.

None of this is necessary.

With just the tiniest addition of computing power, your smart thermostat could learn your home and patterns without ever telling its corporate home a thing. Ditto for everything else on that previous list; even the devices that listen all the time for a key word like *Siri* or *Alexa* could perform most of their work without delivering massive data streams to distant server farms for multidecade storage.

Nonetheless, these devices all pretty much require you to reveal mind-boggling amounts of data to them if you want them to work.

There are even fitness trackers that incidentally record how often and how vigorously you have sex.[4] And that very data, collected by one of the largest fitness-watch companies, has been used several times now for prosecutions in court, including a rape case.[5]

Big Brother Goes Commercial

Some years ago, my wife, Louise, was diagnosed with breast cancer.

A few days after her biopsy, before she'd even told her mother about it, she noticed that wherever she went on the internet, various unrelated websites were throwing ads at her for wigs and special bras for women who'd had breast surgery.

When she joined me in the afternoon in our radio studio, a few miles from the boat we lived on in Washington, DC, websites she viewed on the computers there did the same thing.

All she had to do was log in to her email or pretty much any other account with her name or email attached to it (retailers, the hospital where they'd done the biopsy, the website for paying our utilities, etc.), and the stalking began.

Like magic, website after website—almost all news sites, as she used these computers to produce our show—would toss ads to her pitching everything from herbs and drugs for dealing with chemo sickness to bras, wigs, and specialized cancer treatment centers.

Even worse, as the computers at the TV studio we worked at in the evening were shared with other people, the cancer-related ads would persist long after Louise had logged out and other people were using the same computer.

Not knowing about her diagnosis, one person at the network made a joke about Louise searching for wigs (something, at that time, she'd never done in her life) as if she were trying to upgrade her appearance.

Thankfully Louise is fine, but our first real in-your-face encounter with what was probably just simple cookie-based internet tracking was a wake-up call. It most likely was the result of her doing internet-based research into breast cancer or possibly her email provider reading her email from her physician's office so it could "optimize" advertisements for her.

This was merely embarrassing; it could have been much worse.

COMMERCIAL BIG BROTHER: SO, YOU WANT TO RENT AN APARTMENT?

If Louise had wanted to rent an apartment, her internet usage—and a startling number of other bits of digital data about her—might have been more consequential.

CoreLogic is a "data analytics" company that produces a secret number—secret to renters, anyway—called the Safe-Rent score that uses "the most comprehensive and predictive set of public, contributory and proprietary data" and "analyzes data from multiple sources including application information, eviction history, and credit bureau data to deliver a single score that indicates the risk of each application."[6]

The personal data giant TransUnion offers a similar service, SmartMove, that uses "ResidentScore to predict rental eviction risk 15% better than traditional credit scores, helping landlords make a more confident rental decision."[7]

These services seem benign; after all, what person renting out their property to strangers wouldn't want to know if those strangers had a criminal background, had skipped out on a bunch of previous rentals, or had recently lost their job?

The challenge comes when their data is wrong or incomplete, because everything is compiled and organized in secret. Even the way they compile and interpret the information is a trade secret protected by our courts; as with nearly all the companies that compile your data and produce scores that predict your future behavior, you are simply not allowed to know what they think they know about you because they've labeled the process a "trade secret."

The consumer advocacy group #REPRESENT compiled complaints about these services flagging people as a bad credit risk or as having a criminal history when neither was the case.[8]

Brianda in Glendale, Arizona, for example, reported that her husband had been flagged as a criminal (when, in fact, he'd even passed an FBI fingerprint and background check earlier in the year), resulting in their being unable to rent a home. A real criminal apparently had a similar name, but, she said, "I am not sure how this company works or how they can link two completely different people to provide a bogus report. Very frustrated with them!"[9]

COMMERCIAL BIG BROTHER: SO, YOU'RE LOOKING FOR A JOB?

About three-quarters of all American employers use data that's bought, sold, and extrapolated in secret marketplaces to determine if you'll be a good hire.

HireVue, for example, scores you on "20,000 data points we collect" including "[t]he content of the verbal response, intonation, and nonverbal communication" they find in online videos that have tagged you on social media and other sites.[10]

Cornerstone OnDemand works with some of America's larger employers, like Walgreens, Hyatt, and Wendy's. The oversight group #REPRESENT notes that "Cornerstone's algorithm 'favors lower commute times,'" but all the other data points they use to score you for a potential employer are trade secrets.[11]

COMMERCIAL BIG BROTHER:
SO, YOU WANT TO RETURN A PRODUCT YOU BOUGHT?

One of the oldest retail frauds is for people to shoplift items and then return them to the store for cash, saying they'd bought them but lost the receipt. Like voter fraud, it's something that was once a thing, but in this day and age of computers and credit cards tracking retail activity, it's pretty much nonexistent.

However, as with voter fraud, it's a great excuse to score people, significantly increasing retailers' power in all respects. (There are, of course, other types of retail fraud that are problematic.)

These types of scores are based on thousands of data points that consumers know nothing about, ranging from geolocation data from their phone and car to physical characteristics described on their driver's license to details of their browsing behavior as they surf the web.

Sift is a company that scores consumers using "massive data" and "deep expertise" for companies from Starbucks to OpenTable, Wayfair to Instacart.

"More than 16,000 signals inform the 'Sift score,'" wrote Christopher Mims in the *Wall Street Journal* in 2019. "This score is like a credit score," he added, "but for overall trustworthiness," according to "a company spokeswoman."[12]

If Sift has flagged you as "untrustworthy" for one particular retail outlet, you may not be able to open an account, complete a transaction, or even interact with multiple other retailers.[13]

As the consumer group #REPRESENT noted in a 2019 complaint to the Federal Trade Commission, "Like all Surveillance Scores, the Sift score is a closely-guarded secret."[14]

Other companies offering similar services include the Retail Equation, whose fraud score is used in 34,000 stores in the United States, including Best Buy, Home Depot, and Sephora. Once you're flagged by them, you'll be unable to return products to these stores regardless of how well you document your identity and the money trail to your purchase.

If you've been flagged by another data company, Riskified, "unlike the Retail Equation, whose scores only result in the denial of returns, Riskified's fraud scores go even farther by not only preventing returns of merchandise *but also* [preventing] purchases."[15]

COMMERCIAL BIG BROTHER: SO, YOU WANT TO CALL CUSTOMER SERVICE?

Have you ever tried to call customer service for a company you do business with and ended up on hold for an hour or more? Or, worse, gotten lost repeatedly in a computer-phone maze that ends up refusing to connect you to any human at all?

Welcome to Zeta Global, Kustomer, Opera Solutions, and Affinitiv, companies that determine your "quality" as a customer. High-quality customers get right through (all these companies know your phone number; that's the easiest part), but low-quality customers often never get past the computer.

According to Represent Consumers, Zeta Global "has a database of more than 700 million people, with an average of over 2,500 pieces of data per person."[16] This data includes "the number of times a customer has dialed a [customer service] call center and whether that person has browsed a competitor's website or searched certain keywords in the past few days."[17] Among others, they provide customer scores to mobile phone companies.

Opera Solutions, which provides services to banks, retailers, and airlines (among others), tracks "the number of times a person calls to complain over the prior 90 days," drawing their data from "more than 5,000 data 'signals' per customer."[18]

Affinitiv markets their consumer scoring service to car dealers, among others, and their CEO said their goal is "to weed out costly customers," those being "people who visit 16 stores to get the absolute lowest price."[19]

In all cases, the data on you, the way that data has been gathered, and the way it's evaluated and delivered to the companies you're trying to interact with is a trade secret and unavailable to the average consumer.

COMMERCIAL BIG BROTHER:
SO, YOU WANT TO SHOP FOR THE BEST DEAL?

Perhaps the most egregious abuse of customer scoring shows up when different people with different scores look at the same website offering products or services for sale. Recently, researchers at Northeastern University tested 16 popular e-commerce websites using 300 actual consumers who screen-captured and otherwise documented what they were offered.[20]

Using the Price Discrimination Tool developed by Northeastern researchers, the group Represent Consumers found Home Depot offering five gallons of Glidden Speed-Wall Semi-Gloss Interior Paint for $59.87 or $62.96, depending on who the website thought was viewing it. Similar differences happened across multiple products on the Home Depot site in their 2019 study.[21]

Walmart offered an InterDesign Classico Toilet Paper Roll Holder for $10.26 to one browser, but the same product was $20.89 on their site when the website thought a different consumer was shopping. Bic Gel Pens were either $3.64 or $8.00, Bic Ballpoint pens were either $4.15 or $9.96, and Viva Signature Cloth Paper Towels ran from $12.42 to $16.98.[22]

Christian Bennefeld, founder of etracker.com, the "Google analytics alternative made in Germany," discovered that "there was a $23 difference in Travelocity's prices for the Hotel Le Six in Paris," depending on who was searching for a room.[23]

The Northeastern University Price Discrimination study found similar variations on airfares offered by CheapTickets and Orbitz, while Represent Consumers stated in their FTC complaint that "Expedia and Hotels.com steer a subset of users toward more expensive hotels; and Priceline acknowledges it 'personalizes search results based on a user's history of clicks and purchases.'"[24]

In every case, your score is secret—even its existence is usually not acknowledged—the source, amount, and details of your data are secret, and the algorithm used to evaluate you is secret.

The American free enterprise system has always been promoted as being founded and grounded in the notion of fairness and openness; Big Data has blown that all to hell, separating Americans into thousands of micro-categories that determine the price you pay, the willingness of companies to even engage with you, and your ability to hold companies to account when they mistreat you.

Complaining about being mistreated, in fact, is one of the data points that most of these companies will vacuum up and use to further lower your score.

None of this is disclosed, and the scoring not only can't be challenged (in nearly all cases) but isn't even acknowledged.

And where do they get all this data?

From us.

And then they churn their profits by exploiting a new frontier of our human capital: data that both corporate and governmental Big Brothers find will enhance their power, profit, or both.

The Bottom Line? Your Life Is Profitable

At the United States' founding, its economy was largely built on the exploitation of human beings. Enslaved humans built most of Washington, DC's most iconic buildings, for example, including the White House and our Capitol.

About half of the Founders and Framers acquired and maintained their lifestyle by the merciless utilization of the life energy of others. And the enslaved and exploited people, if they wanted to live, had no say in the matter.

Converting the sum and substance of human life into revenue and profit for an overclass is nothing new; it's at the foundation of both slavery and capitalism going back 7,000 years. Today's data mining industry, while less intrusive, follows that old pattern.

The old joke, that if you don't have to pay for an online product, you *are* the product, barely scratches the surface.

And it's not just to sell you soap.

Big Data monetizes the substance of your life to sell you products, help companies lower risks (from insurance companies that want to know your lifestyle to retailers that want to know if you're a good credit risk), and compile information about you that they can monetize in a variety of ways.

But there can be big consequences for you in each of those categories. While a car dealer may want to know if you've looked at articles on new cars and what kind of credit risk you are, a political party or neo-Nazi group could be looking for behaviors and personality traits that may make you a good recruit.

In 2018, an information technology (IT) specialist in Carrollton, Texas, discovered that his CPAP machine wasn't just keeping track of how well he was breathing at night. It was also sending that information, in detail, to his insurance company, which could use his ease or difficulty breathing at night to determine how high they would push his premiums.[25]

One of the larger customers for Big Data's product is the US government, although spy and police agencies from governments all over the world routinely purchase data on their citizens . . . or the citizens of other countries they'd like to influence.

The Cambridge Analytica scandal blew up when Americans learned that a British Big Data company was working to make Donald Trump president; the tale unraveled when an American, Associate Professor David Carroll at the Parsons School of Design, sued to get the information they had on him.

As the BBC reported, "Prof Carroll was unhappy about how the political marketing firm was using his data, after it was revealed that it had built profiles on up to 240 million Americans and boasted that it had 4,000 to 5,000 data points on each voter."[26]

A 2014 investigation by the Federal Trade Commission (FTC) found that some of the simplest profiles these companies compile on each of us include items such as the following:

• Name • Previously Used Names • Address • Address History • Longitude and Latitude • Phone Numbers • Email Address • Social Security Number • Driver's License Number • Birth Date • Birth Dates of Each Child in Household • Birth Date of Family Members in Household • Age • Height • Weight • Gender • Race and Ethnicity

• Country of Origin • Religion (by Surname at the Household Level) • Language • Marital Status • Presence of Elderly Parent • Presence of Children in Household • Education Level • Occupation • Family Ties • Demographic Characteristics of Family Members in Household • Number of Surnames in Household • Veteran in Household • Grandparent in House • Spanish Speaker • Foreign Language Household (e.g., Russian, Hindi, Tagalog, Cantonese) • Households with a Householder Who Is Hispanic Origin or Latino • Employed—White Collar Occupation • Employed—Blue Collar Occupation • Work at Home • Length of Residence • Household Size • Congressional District • Single Parent with Children • Ethnic and Religious Affiliations • Court and Public Record Data • Bankruptcies • Criminal Offenses and Convictions • Judgments • Liens • Marriage Licenses • State Licenses and Registrations (e.g., Hunting, Fishing, Professional) • Voting Registration and Party • Electronics Purchases • Friend Connections • Internet Connection • Internet Provider • Level of Usage • Heavy Facebook User • Heavy Twitter User • Twitter User with 250+ Friends • Is a Member of over 5 Social Networks • Online Influence • Operating System • Software Purchases • Type of Media Posted • Uploaded Pictures • Use of Long Distance Calling Services • Presence of Computer Owner • Use of Mobile Devices • Social Media and Internet Accounts including: Digg, Facebook, Flickr, Flixster, Friendster, hi5, Hotmail, LinkedIn, Live Journal, MySpace, Twitter, Amazon, Bebo, CafeMom, DailyMotion, Match, myYearbook, NBA.com, Pandora, Photobucket, WordPress, and YahooHome and Neighborhood Data • Census Tract Data • Address Coded as Public/Government Housing • Dwelling Type • Heating and Cooling • Home Equity • Home Loan Amount and Interest Rate • Home Size • Lender Type • Length of Residence • Listing Price • Market Value • Move Date • Neighborhood Criminal, Demographic, and Business Data • Number of Baths • Number of Rooms • Number of Units • Presence of Fireplace • Presence of Garage • Presence of

Home Pool • Rent Price • Type of Owner • Type of Roof • Year •
Apparel Preferences • Attendance at Sporting Events • Charitable
Giving • Gambling—Casinos • Gambling—State Lotteries • Thrifty
Elders • Life Events (e.g., Retirement, Newlywed, Expectant Parent)
• Magazine and Catalog Subscriptions • Media Channels Used •
Participation in Outdoor Activities (e.g., Golf, Motorcycling, Skiing,
Camping) • Participation in Sweepstakes or Contests • Pets • Political
Leanings • Assimilation Code • Preferred Celebrities • Preferred
Movie Genres • Preferred Music Genres • Reading and Listening
Preferences • Donor (e.g., Religious, Political, Health Causes) •
Financial Newsletter Subscriber • Upscale Retail Card Holder •
Affluent Baby Boomer • Working-Class Moms • Working Woman
• African-American Professional • Membership Clubs • Member-
ship Clubs—Wines • Exercise—Sporty Living • Winter Activity
Enthusiast • Participant—Motorcycling • Outdoor/Hunting and
Shooting • Biker/Hell's Angels • Santa Fe/Native American Lifestyle
• New Age/Organic Lifestyle • Is a Member of over 5 Shopping Sites
• Media Channel Usage—Daytime TV • Bible Lifestyle • Leans Left •
Political Conservative • Political Liberal • Activism and Social Issues
• Ability to Afford Products • Credit Card User • Presence of Gold
or Platinum Card • Credit Worthiness • Recent Mortgage Borrower
• Pennywise Mortgagee • Financially Challenged • Owns Stocks or
Bonds • Investment Interests • Discretionary Income Level • Credit
Active • Credit Relationship with Financial or Loan Company •
Credit Relationship with Low-End Standalone Department Store •
Number of Investment Properties Owned • Estimated Income • Life
Insurance • Loans • Net Worth Indicator • Underbanked Indicator
• Tax Return Transcripts • Type of Credit Cards • Vehicle Brand
Preferences • Insurance Renewal • Make & Model • Vehicles Owned •
Vehicle Identification Numbers • Vehicle Value Index • Propensity to
Purchase a New or Used Vehicle • Propensity to Purchase a Particular
Vehicle Type (e.g., SUV, Coupe, Sedan) • Motor Cycle Owner (e.g.,

Harley, Off-Road Trail Bike) • Motor Cycle Purchased 0–6 Months Ago • Boat Owner • Purchase Date • Purchase Information • Intend to Purchase—Vehicle • Read Books or Magazines About Travel • Travel Purchase—Highest Price Paid • Date of Last Travel Purchase • Air Services—Frequent Flyer • Vacation Property • Vacation Type (e.g., Casino, Time Share, Cruises, RV) • Cruises Booked • Preferred Vacation Destination • Preferred Airline • Amount Spent on Goods • Buying Activity • Method of Payment • Number of Orders • Buying Channel Preference (e.g., Internet, Mail, Phone) • Types of Purchases • Military Memorabilia/Weaponry • Shooting Games • Guns and Ammunition • Christian Religious Products • Jewish Holidays/Judaica Gifts • Kwanzaa/African-Americana Gifts • Type of Entertainment Purchased • Type of Food Purchased • Average Days Between Orders • Last Online Order Date • Last Offline Order Date • Online Orders $500–$999.99 Range • Offline Orders $1,000+ Range • Number of Orders—Low-Scale Catalogs • Number of Orders—High-Scale Catalogs • Retail Purchases—Most Frequent Category • Mail Order Responder—Insurance • Mailability Score • Apparel—Women's Plus Sizes • Apparel—Men's Big and Tall • Books—Mind and Body/Self-Help • Internet Shopper • Novelty Elvis • Ailment and Prescription Online Search Propensity • Propensity to Order Prescriptions by Mail • Smoker in Household • Tobacco Usage • Over the Counter Drug Purchases • Geriatric Supplies • Use of Corrective Lenses or Contacts • Allergy Sufferer • Have Individual Health Insurance Plan • Buy Disability Insurance • Buy Supplemental to Medicare/Medicaid Individual Insurance • Brand Name Medicine Preference • Magazines—Health • Weight Loss and Supplements • Purchase History or Reported Interest in Health Topics including: Allergies, Arthritis, Medicine Preferences, Cholesterol, Diabetes, Dieting, Body Shaping, Alternative Medicine, Beauty/Physical Enhancement, Disabilities, Homeopathic Remedies, Organic Focus, Orthopedics, and Senior Needs.[27]

The FTC's snapshot of the industry concluded, in *their* words, the following:

- Data Brokers Collect Consumer Data from Numerous Sources, Largely Without Consumers' Knowledge. . . .

- The Data Broker Industry Is Complex, with Multiple Layers of Data Brokers Providing Data to Each Other: Data brokers provide data not only to end-users, but also to other data brokers. . . .

- Data Brokers Collect and Store Billions of Data Elements Covering Nearly Every U.S. Consumer: Data brokers collect and store a vast amount of data on almost every U.S. household and commercial transaction. Of the nine data brokers, one data broker's database has information on 1.4 billion consumer transactions and over 700 billion aggregated data elements; another data broker's database covers one trillion dollars in consumer transactions; and yet another data broker adds three billion new records each month to its databases. . . .

- Data Brokers Combine and Analyze Data About Consumers to Make Inferences About Them, Including Potentially Sensitive Inferences. . . .

- Data Brokers Combine Online and Offline Data. . . . Once a data broker locates a consumer online and places a cookie on the consumer's browser, the data broker's client can advertise to that consumer across the Internet for as long as the cookie stays

on the consumer's browser. . . . Some data brokers
are using similar technology to serve targeted
advertisements to consumers on mobile devices.[28]

In a section called "Benefits and Risks," the FTC stated the
following:

- Storing Data About Consumers Indefinitely May
  Create Security Risks. . . . For example, identity
  thieves and other unscrupulous actors may be
  attracted to the collection of consumer profiles
  that would give them a clear picture of consumers' habits over time, thereby enabling them to
  predict passwords, challenge questions, or other
  authentication credentials. . . .

- To the Extent Data Brokers Offer Consumers
  Choices About Their Data, the Choices Are
  Largely Invisible and Incomplete.[29]

In 2016, before the door to Facebook's spying on its users
closed, ProPublica provided Facebook users with a tool to discover the "categories of interest" the company had assigned
to them. They reported, "Users showed us everything from
'Pretending to Text in Awkward Situations' to 'Breastfeeding
in Public.' In total, we collected more than 52,000 unique attributes that Facebook has used to classify users."[30]

Cracked Labs, a German outfit, published a report titled
Corporate Surveillance in Everyday Life that contains a graphic
(see Figure 1), describing how granular is the data that these
companies compile on us, from the things we look at online to
how long we look at them to how aggressively we type.[31]

Figure 1. ANALYZING FACEBOOK LIKES, PHONE DATA, AND TYPING PATTERNS

Predicting Personal Attributes from Facebook Likes

PREDICTED ATTRIBUTE	ACCURACY
Ethnicity	95%
Gender	93%
Sexual Orientation (male)	88%
Political Views	85%
Religion	82%
Sexual Orientation (female)	75%
Nicotine Usage	73%
Alcohol Usage	70%
Relationship	67%
Drug Usage	65%
Parents Divorced	60%

Predicting Personal Attributes from Facebook Likes. Source: Kosinski et al., 2013.

Predicting Character Traits from Phone Call Records and App Usage

	EMOTIONAL STABILITY	EXTRA-VERSION	OPENNESS	CONSCIEN-TIOUSNESS	AGREE-ABLENESS
ACCURACY	72%	76%	69%	75%	70%

Source: Chittaranjan et al., 2011

Recognizing Emotions from the Rhythm of Keyboard Typing Patterns

	CONFI-DENCE	HESITANCE	NERVOUS-NESS	RELAX-ATION	SADNESS	TIRED
ACCURACY	83%	82%	83%	77%	88%	84%

Source: Epp et al., 2011

But this isn't just a problem because Data Big Brother is profiting from you and me and we're not sharing in the profits. The much bigger problem is that Data Big Brother is profiting from *changing the way you and I behave.*

Data Big Brother represents something worse than de Tocqueville's "tutelary power,"[32] because Big Data doesn't even try to pretend that it wants to control us to protect us or gives a damn about democracy. Instead, when its message must be made explicit, it says that it wants to *help* us, to make life *more convenient* for us.

The reality, though, is that Data Big Brother exists only to profit by selling the most advanced and sophisticated social control tools that have ever existed. We're allowing these companies to sell out our privacy and even our democracy (remember Facebook and Trump) for no other reason than to deliver profits to their shareholders.

Surveillance and Social Control: We Change When We're Watched

Surveillance as a way to modify behavior didn't start with *Big Brother* the reality show, *The Truman Show*, or even George Orwell's dystopian society in *1984*.

In 1791, when George Washington was in his second year as the first president of the new United States of America, British polymath and philosopher Jeremy Bentham published his idea for a new type of prison, using a concept he thought could eventually extend to hospitals, schools, and factories.

The key to Bentham's invention, which he called the "panopticon," was his belief that people's behavior would change for the better when they knew they could be observed at any particular random time. Thus, his proposed panopticon prison was built as a giant circle, with all the cells facing inward toward an observation center, where guards could, without being seen themselves, watch and randomly monitor their prisoners' behavior.

Although the idea never caught on with prisons (a few tried), Bentham was onto something.

In 1979, researchers published a study titled "Self-Awareness and Transgression in Children" that showed how "[s]elf-awareness induced by the presence of a mirror placed behind the candy bowl decreased transgression rates."[33] A subsequent study with a slightly different method found the same result.

The "observer effect" is why field researchers observing animals go out of their way to be invisible or at least as discreet as possible.

And it's true of humans as well. Back in 2006, researchers positioned themselves in the emergency ward of a mental hospital to observe how new medications might change the behavior of severely agitated patients. What they discovered was that when those patients were being observed, the need for sedative injections to control their behavioral outbursts dropped by 27 percent—regardless of the medication they were on.[34]

Examples of how the observer effect—and the absence of it—alters our behavior occasionally burst into the news, such as when a noted American legal scholar began to watch pornography and masturbate during a break in a Zoom conference, mistakenly believing his camera was turned off.

A nearly universal memory for most people is how, as children, their behavior in a classroom changed when the teacher left the room; replacing the observer teacher with observer students often produces significant alterations in behavior, and both are different from the unobserved state.

Researchers at the University of Newcastle in the UK tested the hypothesis that putting up signs with pictures of eyes and the words "Cycle Thieves—We Are Watching You!" would reduce the widespread nuisance crime of bicycle theft.

The signs cut theft by 62 percent, leading the researchers to conclude, "The effectiveness of this extremely cheap and simple intervention suggests that there can be considerable crime-reduction benefits to engaging the psychology of surveillance, even in the absence of surveillance itself."[35]

The researchers followed up this study with another one using the *same* signs, printed as flyers, attached to handlebars with rubber bands to see if the signs with visible eyes (even though they were warning against bike theft) would reduce people's littering when disposing of the flyers. Sure enough, compared with papers that had no eyes, they worked.[36]

Adding to the cooling effect, Americans are now learning just how revealing private information can be—even when the companies that compile and sell it strip out personal identifying information. This became clear in July 2021 when Monsignor Jeffrey Burrill, the general secretary of the United States Conference of Catholic Bishops and leader of a campaign to deny Communion to President Biden, was outed for using the Grindr app to organize gay hookups.

The news site that outed Monsignor Burrill, *The Pillar*, bought the anonymized data from a broker selling Grindr data and overlaid it with similarly anonymized cell phone information they'd bought from data brokers for cell phone companies serving the area where Burrill lived.

The Pillar announced on their site that "an analysis of app data signals correlated to Burrill's mobile device" showed that he "visited gay bars and private residences while using a location-based hookup app in numerous cities from 2018 to 2020, even while traveling on assignment for the U.S. bishops' conference." They added that Burrill had been doing this "on a near-daily basis during parts of 2018, 2019, and 2020—at both his USCCB office and his USCCB-owned residence, as well as during USCCB meetings and events in other cities."[37]

Burrill resigned, and across America, users of hookup apps had a collective "WTF?!" moment.

Which raises the question, what impact does everybody being observed almost all the time, and knowing it, have on democracy itself?

Social Control and Social Cooling

Dutch artist, technology critic, and privacy designer Tijmen Schep coined the term *social cooling* to describe how people downregulate their behavior, from partying to surfing the web to participating in politics, when they realize that Big Data is watching them.[38]

Schep argues that Big Data drives social cooling in a manner similar to the way Big Oil drives global warming. And, he submits, just as global warming could destroy human civilization, social cooling can destroy democracy.[39]

He defines three specific areas of concern: a culture of conformity, a culture of risk aversion, and increased social rigidity. As people become more aware that their every click and keystroke is logged, Schep says, they become more cautious and begin to self-censor. As an example, he cites a *New York Times* story about how teenagers during spring break have radically scaled back their rowdy, drunken, and publicly sexual activity for fear that friends will capture it on a cell phone camera and post it on social media.

"They are more polite and they wait their turn," one Key West bartender told the *Times*. "One in 10 still acts like spring breakers, but it's definitely calmer than when I was on spring break in 2004."[40]

Dictatorial and repressive regimes across the planet, from China to Saudi Arabia to the Philippines, rely on their own well-known surveillance systems to cause people to self-censor pro-democracy political views, making those views seem rare in those societies. Without the social backstop of peer agreement, people begin to abandon such views altogether.

Noting that "social pressure is the most powerful and most subtle form of control," Schep points to China's "social credit score," which is based on everything from police files to activity online to retail purchases and "even the scores of their friends."[41] In a chilling codicil he says, "If you have a low score you can't get a government job, visa, cheap loan, or even a nice online date." (See "Are We Doomed to Live Under Big Brother's Watchful Eye?" in part 4 for more on this.)

How much power and social control does a small group of people hold when they control the data and the algorithms for that social credit score? Enough to subvert even the staunch-est of democratic countries.

Big Data: Surveillance Monopolists

A few weeks ago, I needed a new tablet to monitor the video feed of my TV show, which is carried by the Free Speech TV network via the online-TV app Sling (among other sources). RCA was offering a cheap little seven-inch unit for about $70, so I ordered it, and when it arrived, I set it up. The operating system was Android, which is owned by Alphabet, the com-pany that owns Google.

All I bought this tablet for was to run the Sling app, so when I set up the initial connection to my home Wi-Fi, I ignored/skipped/said no to all the requests that I use my Google account to sign in so that they could track everything I said or did online.

Until I tried to get the app. For that, I had to go to the Goo-gle Play online store app, and before the system would let me download Sling's app, it required me to sign in. Gotcha! Now Google is tracking everything that happens on that little tablet.

Google, of course, isn't unique in this. When I want to install an app on the Apple computer I'm using to write this book, I have to sign in to Apple so that they can keep track of me.

And my word processor, Microsoft Word, has switched from a "buy the software disc and it's yours to use as and where you want" business model to a "pay us a licensing fee every year and be continuously connected to the Microsoft servers" model. I don't know what they're doing with my information (or if they're reading these words as I type them), but I'm not optimistic.

How is it that a search engine company gets to track every app I install on my tablet computer? Or a computer hardware company? Or an operating system company?

And how does this Big Brother activity all relate to an overall loss of our privacy?

Turns out, the power of scale that enables this and the political power to prevent government or even consumers from doing anything about it largely derive from a single source, which is not technological. It's monopoly.

We can track today's tech giants' power straight back to a 1983 decision made by the Reagan administration to largely stop enforcing antitrust laws passed from the 1890s through the 1970s, as well as the Supreme Court's later adopting the same perspective, promoted by Reagan's adviser Robert Bork.

As these companies got bigger and bigger, wiping out and buying up competitors, their market share and thus their ability to aggregate massive amounts of data reached a tipping point that made them essentially unstoppable. Along with that market share came billions in revenue that could be weaponized to lift up or take out politicians who supported or opposed their business model.

Just 60 years ago this would have been unthinkable.

In the 1962 antitrust case of *Brown Shoe Co. v. United States*, for example, the US Supreme Court blocked the merger of Brown and G. R. Kinney, two shoe manufacturers, because the combination of the two would have captured about 5 percent of the US shoe market.

Similarly, there was a time when anti-monopoly laws and the Supreme Court wouldn't tolerate either vertical or horizontal integration of a company.

In the early years of the movie industry, for example, the big movie companies also owned the theaters in which their movies were shown. If you wanted to watch a Paramount movie, you had to go to a Paramount-owned theater.

The Supreme Court got into the act in 1948 in *United States v. Paramount Pictures* and declared that such vertical integration was an unlawful form of monopoly. In the process, they opened up an explosion of competition in both industries (moviemaking and movie showing) and began the end of the old studio system.

Similarly, the 1970 Prime Time Access Rule and Financial Interest and Syndication Rules from the Federal Communications Commission (FCC) busted open TV's evening hours between 7 and 11 p.m. on the East Coast.[42] The prime time rule required that local stations carry minimum amounts of programming that wasn't produced by the networks that owned or had an affiliation agreement with the stations. The so-called fin-syn rule even required the networks themselves to make available to their stations programming in prime time that wasn't produced or owned by the networks, which had previously locked up this most valuable block of time.

The result of the rule changes was a proliferation of competition and creativity. One of the first non-network-owned companies to offer quality programming for that block was started and owned by TV star Mary Tyler Moore, also a savvy businesswoman. Her company, MTM Enterprises, brought to the small screen *Rhoda, Lou Grant, Phyllis, The Bob Newhart*

Show, The Texas Wheelers, WKRP in Cincinnati, The White Shadow, Friends and Lovers, St. Elsewhere, Newhart, Hill Street Blues, and, of course, *The Mary Tyler Moore Show.*

By confining companies to specific market niches (making movies, showing movies, making TV shows, broadcasting those shows, etc.), antitrust law as enforced by the US Supreme Court until the 1980s kept companies to a reasonable size and promoted vigorous competition. Since the Reagan Revolution, though, that's pretty much fallen apart (there's a deep dive into this in the *Hidden History* books about the Supreme Court and monopolies).

While core privacy protections must be put into place and enforced—the European Union has begun this, as has the state of California—the most important way to recover some semblance of our privacy is to break up the Big Brother internet behemoths.

The result of such a breakup would be a far more competitive and less leveraged internet landscape where one company makes and sells hardware, another company produces operating systems, another creates browsers, another runs a search engine, another sells and places advertising, etc.

The problem with putting this solution into place is how both the Supreme Court and conservatives in Congress have interpreted antitrust laws over the past 40 years. Robert Bork, a student in the 1950s of Milton Friedman, whose financial patrons were the largest of American companies, spent much of his professional career promoting the idea that our anti-monopoly laws had to be watered down and replaced with his "brilliant" new idea.

A giant corporation, or a small group of giant corporations that had come to dominate more than 70 percent of an industry, wasn't a monopoly, Bork said, if it didn't produce increases in prices to the consumer. Instead of looking at market dominance, ability to block out competition, or any of the other variables that had traditionally been part of government regulators' concluding that a monopoly existed, Bork said that one element, consumer pricing, was the singular variable that everybody from the Federal Trade Commission to the Justice Department to the US Supreme Court should concern themselves with.

Reagan adopted Bork's logic, as did the Court in the 1980s, and it's all been downhill ever since. Today there's not a single industry that's not dominated by three to five major corporations that typically work in lockstep just on the legal edge of collusion. The most obvious result, as I document in *The Hidden History of Monopolies*, is that the average American family pays around $5,000 a year more than the average European family for everything from food to medicine to phone service and internet access. I call it the "monopoly tax," although instead of going to the government to be used for the public good, it goes right into corporate coffers.

Witness, for example, how if Delta changes their airfare on a particular route, United will match that change within hours. It's all arm's-length wink-and-nod, but regardless of what you call it, it's anti-competitive and meets all the classic definitions of monopoly/oligopoly.

For capitalism to work in a way that doesn't produce oligarchs and monopolies, it must be regulated. Capitalism, after all, is just a game that people play using money and mutually agreed-upon rules.

A good analogy is football. The NFL regulates football in the United States, at least the football played by its teams. Those regulations include how many players are on the field at any time, exactly what constitutes a down or a touchdown, and rules about how players may physically contact each other and under what circumstances.

The NFL's regulations also decide which team gets first pick of new players: they decided that the worst-performing teams should have first choice of newly available players, giving every team an opportunity to rise up through the ranks in the following season. It's sort of like progressive taxation, giving the little guy a chance while slightly restraining those already at the top.

These regulations guarantee the safety and stability of the game itself, and also guarantee that fans of football have a consistent experience, because everybody understands and follows the rules.

But imagine if Milton Friedman, Robert Bork, or the other fabulists like them who advised the Reagan administration had taken over the NFL.

The teams with the wealthiest owners would always get the best players and thus would win every game. They might even decide that the team that gave the executives running the NFL the most money could have an extra player or two on the field at various times.

They would assure us that the teams that didn't perform as well just had to pull themselves up by their bootstraps. Perhaps their problem was just that their players were lazy, these people would tell us, and the solution was to cut their salaries and reduce the amount of protective equipment they could wear so that they would have an incentive to play harder and increase their performance.

Then the richest teams would begin buying the poorer teams, until all the teams were owned by three or four billionaires. Sounds like a football paradise, right?

It's actually a pretty good description of what's been happening in the internet/data/social media sector since the 1990s as it's come to be dominated by a handful of Big Brother corporations.

Comcast and three other companies own more than 70 percent of the internet service provider (ISP) niche, Google stands alone in search, Microsoft and Apple own the operating system space, and Facebook and Twitter are unchallenged in social media.

It's argued that breaking up the Big Data giants would simply produce a plethora of smaller companies all equally enthusiastic about ruining our privacy. But without the massive databases that a single company like Google or Facebook can compile, the market for data would rapidly specialize into niches that were easier to identify, regulate, and—when a person wanted—avoid or opt out of.

Beyond that, it would de-concentrate the Big Brother power that these companies currently have, both to influence our behaviors and to profit from selling access to data sets about our behaviors that can be used by others to modify our behaviors.

PART THREE

Big Brother and the Real Global Info Wars

Privacy, Cybersecurity, National Security, and the Future of Warfare

Privacy and safety (or at least a sense of safety) are often intertwined. Given that the deadliest predators humans have faced throughout our history have been members of our own species, it just makes sense.

If you're sitting comfortably in your living room reading a book or watching TV and happen to look up at your front window and see a menacing-looking person standing outside staring at you, you immediately go from feeling safe to feeling unsafe.

Most people don't have deep, dark online secrets they want to hide from others on the internet; most of us are not pornographers or terrorists or burglars. But even the most innocent, benign person would prefer that strangers aren't reading their emails or knowing every click or purchase that comes out of their time online.

Governments, though, are another matter. There isn't a government in the world that doesn't have secrets that, if revealed, would damage the national security of that country. Be it military, trade, or political, governments routinely conceal information for reasons both bad and good, and competing governments are *always* trying to find them out.

Spying, in this regard, is as old as humankind.

From Moses' 12 spies in the Bible to the story of the giant wooden horse that carried warriors into Troy to tales from behind the lines in World War II, we're all familiar with the damage that can be done to a nation when it's infiltrated by hostile agents. And this is where our Internet of Things presents a particular vulnerability for the United States.

On the internet, maintaining privacy and security is important for individuals but vital for governments.

Most Americans are familiar with the story of how the United States and Israel apparently collaborated to implant a computer worm known as Stuxnet into the nuclear enrichment systems of Iran in 2010. The worm burrowed into the computerized systems controlling the spinning centrifuges used to purify uranium, causing them to spin so fast or irregularly that they essentially broke into pieces.[1]

Far less well known is the story of how Iran responded.

A paper from the Strategic Studies Institute of the US Army War College titled *Iran's Emergence as a Cyber Power* states that prior to then, virtually all of that country's cyber capability was directed at spying on their own citizens, hoping to stop rebellions before they began. But Stuxnet changed everything.

"Today, Iran as a cyber power is the elephant in the room that everyone is finally beginning to notice," the report's authors wrote. "The Iranian government was originally believed to have budgeted approximately $76 million annually to its fledgling cyber force."

Then came Stuxnet in 2010. As the War College said, "However, in late-2011, Iran invested at least $1 billion dollars [*sic*] in cyber technology, infrastructure, and expertise. In March 2012, the IRGC [Iran Revolutionary Guard Corps] claimed it had recruited around 120,000 personnel over the past 3 years to combat 'a soft cyber war against Iran.' In early-2013, an IRGC general publicly claimed Iran had the 'fourth biggest cyber power among the world's cyber armies.'"[2]

On August 15, 2012, they used that power first to disable the world's wealthiest oil company, Saudi Aramco, irretrievably destroying 30,000 computers, leaving only an image of a burning American flag on every monitor's screen.

Then they went after a 245-foot-tall, 800-foot-long dam in Oregon, the Arthur R. Bowman Dam, which backs up the Crooked River. Had they opened its floodgates fast enough, it would have wiped out the downriver town of Pineville, killing thousands.

Fortunately for Oregonians, they got the wrong dam; instead of the Oregon dam, they successfully infiltrated and took control of the Bowman Avenue Dam in New York State, which reroutes a relatively small stream. And, to add insult to injury for the Iranians, when they hit that dam (as the CIA was just then discovering), the sluice gates had been separated from the computer system for maintenance.

In an article about the attack, *Wall Street Journal* reporter Danny Yadron wrote, "America's power grid, factories, pipelines, bridges and dams—all prime targets for digital armies—are sitting largely unprotected on the Internet." It was just a fluke that they got the wrong dam *and* that it was down for repairs.[3]

The late Las Vegas billionaire Sheldon Adelson, then a close friend of Benjamin Netanyahu and a major donor to both Israeli and GOP causes, was the next victim of Iran after telling an audience at Yeshiva University in New York that the United States should drop an atomic bomb in Iran's desert, implicitly threatening the capital, Tehran.

"You want to be wiped out? Go ahead and take a tough position," Adelson said.

Iran's Supreme Leader Ayatollah Ali Khamenei replied that somebody "should slap these prating people in the mouth."[4]

Weeks later, all the computers at the Sands, Adelson's hotel/casino, died. Totally. Every hard drive wiped, every screen showing a photo of Adelson and Netanyahu with the inscription, "Don't let your tongue cut your throat"; the computers may as well have been boat anchors. *Bricked* is the word that hackers use.

Two years earlier, the Obama administration had put forward legislation to require all privately owned "essential infrastructure" in the United States to harden their cyber capabilities. While it passed the House of Representatives, as the *New York Times* reported, "Senate Republicans . . . argued that the minimum standards were too burdensome for businesses, and by late July had managed to change the legislation to make them optional. In early August, the bill essentially died when it was blocked by a Republican filibuster."[5]

Failing at getting Congress to force the American companies that controlled our infrastructure to harden their systems, President Obama signed an executive order "that promotes increased information sharing about cyberthreats between the government and private companies that oversee the country's critical infrastructure" and "put together recommendations that companies should follow to prevent attacks."[6]

The order was ignored, and continues to be ignored, by American industry.

Cybersecurity for our privately owned dams, bridges, electrical generating stations, nuclear power plants, gas and oil pipelines, and water and sewage systems is now optional, and few companies—at least until ransomware attacks began in earnest in 2020—invested anything close to the necessary funds to protect against an internet-based attack.

New York Times reporter Nicole Perlroth, in her vital and brilliant book *This Is How They Tell Me The World Ends: The Cyberweapons Arms Race*, wrote that from 2012 to 2014, "Russian hackers made their way inside more than a thousand companies, in more than eighty-four countries, the vast majority of them American."[7]

While the Chinese have hacked American companies for decades and stolen what Perlroth documents as trillions of dollars' worth of intellectual property, product designs, manufacturing techniques, and drug formulas, this Russian hack seemed to have a different purpose.

They "made their way into hundreds of industrial control systems across the country," Perlroth wrote, using systems and strategies similar to the way Stuxnet had penetrated Iranian nuclear enrichment facilities.

"It wasn't just US oil and gas companies anymore," she said. "Russian hackers infected the software updates that reached the industrial controllers inside hydroelectric dams, nuclear power plants, pipelines, and the grid, and were now inside the very computers that could unleash the locks at the dams, trigger an explosion, or shut down power to the grid."

This action "was not Chinese-style industrial espionage," Perlroth wrote. "Moscow was preparing the battlefield."

She quotes cybersecurity expert John Hultquist, who told her, "This was the first stage in long-term preparation for an attack. There's no other plausible explanation."[8]

While a handful of nations with nuclear weapons have spent much of the past 70 years both preparing for and trying to avoid a nuclear war, cyberwar has emerged as a far more likely way the next major international conflict will go down. A few decades ago, neutron bombs were all the rage in the press—weapons that would kill all the people through a massive radiation pulse but leave the infrastructure standing and waiting to be occupied and used or looted by victorious foreign troops.

Cyberwar is sort of the opposite of neutron bombs. Instead of killing the people, it takes out the infrastructure with the goal being to disrupt society so severely as to bring down governments (the ultimate goal of most warfare).

Like a previously unknown and still largely invisible fourth dimension, digital cyberspace has gone from being nonexistent when I was born to having interpenetrated almost every home, business, and government agency in the developed world and most of the developing world. Today everything from our water/power/sewer utilities to our cellular telephone systems to our home information and entertainment systems runs on digital ones and zeros that flow through cyberspace.

And just as the United States and Russia were first into outer space, they—and now China—have become the major players in cyberspace. Rather than the next war starting with a flash from a nuclear explosion over New York or Moscow or Beijing, it's more likely that today the first step would be one of those cities browning out as the electrical grid was fried the way the United States and Israel took out Iran's centrifuges a decade ago. Take out a few big dams and melt down a couple dozen nuclear reactors while shutting down communications systems for first responders, and the country would be thrown into a chaos not unlike the firebombing of Dresden or Tokyo in 1944, but without the expense, hassle, or waste of building, fueling, and flying bombers and bombs.

With no power, no telecommunications, and no water, cities would descend into chaos in days and become unlivable hellscapes within a week; drain the big banks and vanish their depositors' records, and you've hit a nation at all levels from the top government/corporate to infrastructure to the individual and personal.

The risk/reward calculation for cyberwar is so much better than for nuclear war that it's probable that nuclear warfare has become an anachronism and cyberwar is the new military frontier. Every new military weapon ever devised has made its way into warfare within two generations, from the crossbow in the 12th century (two popes tried to ban it) to guns to poison gas to nuclear bombs dropped on Hiroshima and Nagasaki. Cyberwar will be no different as digital Big Brothers battle each other from safe, distant computer terminals while civilian populations and military operations collapse. Conceivably, a nation's own nuclear arsenal could be used against it by programming nuclear bombs and missiles to explode in place.

Multiple nations are today planning for exactly this kind of warfare scenario, and it's already been tried in more local ways, as mentioned earlier with our operations against Iran and Russia's against Ukraine and Estonia, and while the United States took down Saddam Hussein's power and telecommunications through strategic bombing prior to a larger bombing campaign of Baghdad in 2003, the post-2020s version of that strike will most likely be in cyberspace.

How Trump Undermined Our Cybersecurity

A few years before the Russian action, right after taking office in 2009, President Obama gave a speech revealing that both his and Senator John McCain's campaigns had been hacked, as was his personal credit card.

He kicked off a robust new agency within the White House to coordinate cybersecurity across federal agencies so that America wouldn't get caught flat-footed like we were on 9/11 when the FBI and CIA both had essential parts of the Bin Laden puzzle but failed to connect the dots.

J. Michael Daniel was Obama's head of the office of the Cybersecurity Coordinator and special assistant to the president, working with a substantial team out of the Eisenhower Executive Office Building next door to the White House. All the bells and alarms from more than 20 US security agencies, from those associated with the military to the FBI, CIA, NSA, and parts of the government that don't even have public names, coordinated with his operation.

They watched with horror as the day before Christmas Eve, the busiest shopping day of 2015, Russia took down Ukraine a year after voters in that country had expelled a Russian-friendly oligarch, Viktor Yanukovych, and replaced him with a Western-friendly president, Oleksandr Turchynov.

And by "take down," I mean it almost literally. Kim Zetter told the story of a supervisor at one of Ukraine's main power substations in *Wired*: "All he could do was stare helplessly at his screen while the ghosts in the machine clicked open one breaker after another, eventually taking about 30 substations offline. The attackers didn't stop there, however. They also struck two other power distribution centers at the same time, nearly doubling the number of substations taken offline and leaving more than 230,000 residents in the dark. And as if that weren't enough, they also disabled backup power supplies to two of the three distribution centers, leaving operators themselves stumbling in the dark."[9]

It was the second consequential cyberattack (the first being Stuxnet) of one nation-state against another. Prior hacks, mostly by Iran, North Korea, and China, were designed to extort money via ransomware, steal money directly from people's bank accounts or credit cards, or steal product designs and other intellectual properties that could be converted to profit.

But there was no profit motive here, nor in the Stuxnet attack. Both were acts of war.

The United States still had the most powerful cyberweapons in the world, but the Russians were no slouches. For example, back in 2007 when the Estonians (a former Soviet state) removed an old Soviet-era statue from a public square, Russian hackers pulled the internet plug on the entire nation; for a brief while, no traffic got in or out of the country.[10]

In 2016, the US cyberwarfare equivalents of our nuclear arsenal were hacked from our intelligence agencies (particularly the NSA) and put up for sale on the dark web. One of those cybernukes, named by the NSA EternalBlue, was integrated into a new cyberweapon now known as NotPetya and used a year later, June 27, 2017, against Ukraine.

As Andy Greenberg wrote for *Wired*: "On a national scale, NotPetya was eating Ukraine's computers alive. It would hit at least four hospitals in Kiev alone, six power companies, two airports, more than 22 Ukrainian banks, ATMs and card payment systems in retailers and transport, and practically every federal agency. 'The government was dead,' summarizes Ukrainian minister of infrastructure Volodymyr Omelyan."[11]

About 10 percent of all the computers in Ukraine were bricked, permanently destroyed, and more than 300 companies were shut down and lost everything on their computer systems. Checkout systems in stores shut down; gas stations couldn't process payments, so their pumps stopped working; banks went down, and not only were people unable to access their balances, but some banking information (and thus money in the banks) was simply lost, forever.

The cyberweapon even took down the monitoring systems at Chernobyl, provoking mass consternation among the scientists working remotely on the cleanup who didn't know for hours if the site had exploded, been attacked, or just been hacked with devastating consequences.

The response of the Trump administration took a few months but was decisive: In early 2018, Trump shut down the White House Office of the Cybersecurity Coordinator and ended the job of its then-director, Rob Joyce.

In the understatement of the year, Senator Mark Warner of Virginia tweeted, "Mr. President, if you really want to put America first, don't cut the White House Cybersecurity Coordinator, the only person in the federal government tasked with delivering a coordinated, whole-of-government response to the growing cyber threats facing our nation. . . . I don't see how getting rid of the top cyber official in the White House does anything to make our country safer from cyber threats."[12]

An aide to National Security Adviser John Bolton explained, using language lifted from Alexander Hamilton's 1788 *Federalist*, no. 70, that they killed off the cybersecurity czar's office because "eliminating another layer of bureaucracy delivers greater 'decision, activity, secrecy and despatch *[sic]*.'"[13]

After the two years during which Trump forbade America a cybersecurity coordinator, the incoming Biden administration discovered that Russian hackers had used that time to embed themselves deeply into the computer systems of the Treasury and Commerce departments, and nobody as of this writing is sure how far or how deep the Russian hackers went into other government agencies, including our military and intelligence agencies.

They were inside US government computers for almost a year before an outside company, FireEye, discovered the hack and alerted both the government and the media. And there's every indication that they're still there.[14]

When the Russian penetration deep into the US government's computers hit the papers, Trump had, a month earlier, also fired Christopher Krebs, head of the Department of Homeland Security's Cybersecurity Agency (because he'd publicly said there was no fraud in the 2020 election), so that agency was in a bind when the news came out.[15]

FireEye, SolarWinds, and several of America's intelligence agencies unequivocally said the attack was launched from Russia, and Secretary of State Mike Pompeo declared, "This was a very significant effort, and I think it's the case that now we can say pretty clearly that it was the Russians that engaged in this activity."[16]

But President Donald Trump, having now lost the office that Putin had first helped him win in 2016, and a month away from having to vacate the White House, had a different story. The AP reported on December 19, 2020, "Contradicting his secretary of state and other top officials, President Donald Trump on Saturday suggested without evidence that China— not Russia—may be behind the cyber espionage operation against the United States and tried to minimize its impact."[17]

Trump then tweeted, "The Cyber Hack is far greater in the Fake News Media than in actuality. I have been fully briefed and everything is well under control." He accused the media of being "petrified" of "discussing the possibility that it may be China (it may!)."[18]

The headline at *Business Insider* neatly summarized the day: "The White House was set to accuse Russia of the devastating cyberattack on the US government's computer systems but was told at the last minute to stand down."[19] The order apparently came directly from Trump.

The Biden administration began the difficult, expensive, and time-consuming task of rebuilding our cybersecurity infrastructure, but Trump left behind massive damage and what may end up being a years-long Russian presence inside our systems.

America now has a new Big Brother in Russia and probably China as well. Not to mention the Big Data companies that were more than happy to profit from making Trump president and then conceal from the American people exactly how their algorithms worked and what ads they allowed on their platforms.

As we rebuild our cybersecurity infrastructure, it's critical to do so in a way that not only evicts foreign actors but also protects Americans from Big Data's craven actions that regularly put profit above the well-being of the American people and the integrity of our republic.

When Big Brother's Marketing Is Concentrated to Lethal Levels

Earlier I described how the Trump campaign tested more than 150,000 variations of a single ad on a single day during his 2016 campaign against Hillary Clinton to come up with a few thousand versions that most successfully targeted specific types of people. While this may, on its surface, seem nefarious, it's actually just a much faster and more efficient version of what advertisers have been doing for over a century (and probably longer).

In the early 1970s, I was a partner with the late Terry O'Connor in a small Michigan advertising agency, Ter Graphics, and a copywriter for another, Barden-Durst, run by the late Bob Strand. Our biggest clients were Kellogg's and Michigan National Bank, and I learned the business from these men and from in-person instruction by the legendary Joe Sugarman, to whom I'm grateful to this day.

Later in the '70s, I taught marketing and advertising for the American Marketing Centers and in 1989 started the Atlanta advertising agency Chandler, MacDonald, Stout, Schneiderman & Poe, named after my favorite writers and my best friend, which Louise and I sold in 1997 to retire to the mountains of Vermont. CMSS&P primarily did business as the Newsletter Factory, and our clients included more than 100 of the Fortune 500 companies at that time, as well as government agencies from the US Army to the NSA and the CIA.

I say all this not by way of bragging but hopefully to convince you that I know something about the advertising and marketing business.

In addition to producing in-house employee and external marketing newsletters and magazines for companies from Scientific Atlanta to Holiday Inns, we held one-day $265 workshops all over the nation on how to produce high-impact advertising and publications. In a typical year we'd drop around four million pieces of bulk mail to advertise our workshops.

Lamar Waldron, with whom I later wrote two books about the John F. Kennedy assassination (made into an NBC/ History Channel special and praised by Kennedy's friend Gore Vidal in his autobiography), was in charge of these mailings and kept meticulous spreadsheets noting every little change we did in every mailing. A single mailing to a single city might include dozens of versions of our flyer, as we tested copy, headlines, and even typefaces and paper colors across thousands of iterations over the years we ran that company.

Testing dozens of versions of a single magazine ad in multiple publications, or multiple regions and local versions of a newspaper or magazine, was normal then; by the 1960s, people like David Ogilvy had helped turn advertising and marketing from gut-instinct work into a finely honed science based on predictably replicable data.

Thus, the Trump campaign and its allied super PAC doing hundreds of thousands of "A-B" tests and tweaks to optimize them for microtargeted audiences is nothing new. It's now pretty much the norm, in fact, particularly for ads designed for social media.

Gathering information to compile targeted lists of potential customers is nothing new, either. Every one of those four-million-a-year flyers we sent out went to mailing lists we'd rented, typically lists of just a few thousand people each, varying based on a whole spectrum of personal details from job title to age to their having been customers of other advertising-training-related books, products, or workshops.

We were doing what Trump's campaign did, and we were getting our data from list brokers who were doing what Facebook does, albeit a version that was much slower and far less precise.

There's a lot of concern, sometimes bordering on hysteria, about "surveillance capitalism," but the reality is that predicting and selling people's future behavior (particularly their purchasing behavior) based on their past behaviors and life experiences is as old as marketing itself.

What's new is the speed and precision that social media and high-powered computers bring to the game.

Consider this analogy.

We all have opiate receptors in our brain that modulate our response to pain. Compounds that bind to these receptors are produced naturally by our body in response to extreme pain and shock, and numerous plants—most famously, opium poppies—naturally produce chemicals that bind to and activate our opiate receptors.

When we lived in Germany back in the late 1980s, I loved to visit a nearby castle in Kulmbach and order *mohnkuchen*, a piecrust filled with poppy seeds ground with sugar and a few spices. I always felt so *good* after eating a slice or two of the pie, and when we had a glass of a fresh German Riesling with it, my smile went from ear to ear for hours.

The *mohnkuchen* seemed to constipate me a bit, and when I noticed one afternoon that my pupils were pinned so small as to nearly vanish, the same as I'd noticed whenever I'd taken narcotic painkillers after injuries and surgery, the penny dropped. Turns out I was enjoying opium in that little German café in a way that people around the world have for millennia.

Similarly, I once shared a few days with a shaman from Peru; he had a bag of coca leaves, and we each chewed a few along with a tiny piece of alkalized ash to release its active ingredient as an afternoon pick-me-up. The buzz I experienced was considerably *less* strong than what a cup of coffee provides. Mountain-dwelling Andean tribes have been doing this for as long as there've been people in the region; they consume coca the way people in India and parts of China consume local tea leaves.

Somewhere on the spectrum from these drugs' original state to becoming increasingly concentrated and purified, a toxic/addictive threshold or tipping point is reached. I never experienced withdrawal symptoms from *mohnkucken*, but I did from the highly concentrated opiate painkillers I took for a few weeks for severe sciatica prior to spinal surgery. It wasn't terrible; a few nights of trouble sleeping and sensitivity to pain and touch, but there it was.

Heroin is concentrated opium poppy. Cocaine is concentrated coca leaf. Substances that are otherwise benign become both potent and deadly when they're super-concentrated.

Being a young person in the advertising business in the 1970s, I remember well the widespread concern generated a few years earlier by the claim that subliminal messages embedded in movies seen at theaters could induce people to buy popcorn or Coke.

In 1957, Vance Packard published *The Hidden Persuaders*, a book that claimed to expose the secret ways the advertising industry slipped persuasion into its messages well below our conscious ability to recognize or filter them out.

That same year, James Vicary claimed to have run a test of the hypothesis at a Fort Lee, New Jersey, movie theater during the film *Picnic*. He claimed that inserting microsecond pictures and commands increased the sales of Coca-Cola by 18 percent and popcorn by a whopping 57 percent.

The story—which Vicary had apparently invented from whole cloth—went viral, even after Vicary's claim was debunked the following year. In 1973, Dr. Wilson B. Key revived Vicary's hysteria, revealing that the word "SEX" was spelled out subliminally in a liquor ad that pictured a cocktail with ice cubes in a whiskey glass. I remember reading Key's book *Subliminal Seduction* and looking at the ad, although I could never quite see the three letters in the drink.[20]

The TV show *Columbo* aired an episode in 1973 titled "Double Exposure," premised on Vicary's and Key's claims, and the next year the FCC proclaimed that subliminal advertising was "contrary to the public interest." Twice over the next decade, Congress tried to outlaw the practice, but each time they were unable to find any credible evidence of the "subliminal effect."[21]

As exciting and dangerous as subliminal advertising seemed to those of us in the business in 1973, it was all a bunch of hooey. While it's true that good advertisements contain multiple elements that ping us below the level of consciousness, and probably always have, none of that is particularly nefarious.

The question we face today is whether the Big Brother corporate dystopia imagined by Packard, Vicary, and Key several decades ago is being realized today by the likes of Cambridge Analytica, Google, and Facebook. Have they fine-tuned persuasion to such scalpel-like precision by compiling terabytes of data on each of us that they can easily and accurately predict our future behavior . . . and sell those predictions to merchandisers and politicians?

Have they turned the coca and poppyseed of generic advertising into the crack and heroin of a new world in which we buy products we would otherwise despise and vote for politicians who want to harm us and our country?

The premise of several books, most famously Shoshana Zuboff's *The Age of Surveillance Capitalism*, is that the massive acquisition of data about each of us, from our use of things like smart doorbells and thermostats to our searches and emails, has created a new type of capitalism that could spell the doom of both democracy and traditional capitalism.

Zuboff's book is brilliant, and the points she makes are both alarming and cogent. That said, I'd argue that what's new here is not the practice of collecting and analyzing information from and about customers and potential customers (or potential viewers of a particular advertisement) but rather the speed, efficiency, and depth of that collection and analysis.

As with the difference between *mohnkuchen* and heroin, coca leaf and crack, the kind of surveillance activity engaged in by social media and search engine companies is similar in type to older forms of market identification and segmentation, but when juiced by artificial intelligence (AI) and top-secret algorithms, it becomes radically more concentrated, distilled, and potent.

This makes for super-effective and -efficient marketing of everything from gadgets to ideas to candidates, as candidate Trump and Cambridge Analytica showed the world in 2016.

Zuboff wrote that what she calls "surveillance capitalism" gives the companies and governments using this technology the power to be "intervening in our experience to shape our behavior in ways that favor surveillance capitalists' commercial outcomes. New automated protocols are designed to influence and modify human behavior at scale as the means of production is subordinated to a new and more complex *means of behavior modification*." (Emphasis hers in all quotes.)

She notes that "only a few decades ago US society denounced mass behavior-modification techniques as unacceptable threats to individual autonomy and the democratic order." Today, however, "the same practices meet little resistance or even discussion as they are routinely and pervasively deployed" to meet the financial goals of those engaging in surveillance capitalism.

This is such a powerful system for modifying our perspectives and behaviors, she argues, that it intervenes in or interferes with our "elemental *right to the future tense*, which accounts for the individual's ability to imagine, intend, promise, and construct a future."[22]

Using my earlier drug analogy, this theft of our "future tense" is not dissimilar to what happens to an unsuspecting person prescribed inappropriately strong painkillers in doses and lengths of time that are far out of proportion to their need.

Soon the person ends up addicted without even realizing it—until they run out of pills, a condition that millions of Americans found themselves in as a result of the Sackler family's company, Perdue, lying about the safety of Oxycontin to push it, particularly in depressed parts of the country, for years.

Zuboff calls surveillance capitalism a "*coup from above*, not an overthrow of the state but rather an overthrow of the people's sovereignty" that represents "a prominent force in the perilous drift toward democratic deconsolidation that now threatens Western liberal democracies."

And apparently Google cofounder and former CEO Eric Schmidt agrees.

In *The Final Report*, by the National Security Commission on Artificial Intelligence (NSCAI), chaired by Schmidt, the commission says of artificial intelligence, "AI is deepening the threat posed by cyber attacks and disinformation campaigns that Russia, China, and others are using to infiltrate our society, steal our data, and interfere in our democracy. The limited uses of AI-enabled attacks to date represent the tip of the iceberg."[23]

Schmidt told Axios reporter Ina Fried, "I think the No. 1 [type of] attacks that our country will have will be precisely disinformation because the cost is so low and the value is so high."[24]

Hello to QAnon and the dozens of other bizarre right-wing theories about Democratic politicians drinking children's blood (an echo of anti-Semitic blood libels going back centuries) and manipulating our elections to turn America into a "socialist" state totally lacking in "freedom."

These conspiracy fantasies (I won't honor them by using the word *theories*) now promoted in the United States by, among others, hostile foreign governments using the power of AI and the internet include assertions that Trump is secretly running the United States or the world, that America hasn't been a nation but instead a corporation since the late 19th century, that vaccines are used for mind control, that carbon pollution is actually *good* for the planet, and that the white "race" is genetically superior to all others.

They make the earlier generation of crackpot theories that the moon landing was faked, evolution is a myth, and the Earth is flat seem quaint.

As a result, neofascist ethnonationalism not only has seized tens of millions of people in the United States but is spreading like a virus across the rest of the world, with political and racial violence in its wake.

Sadly, there is no shortage of politicians in these nations (including ours) who are perfectly willing to stand on the edges of these beliefs and encourage them just to remain in office and thus maintain their proximity to great political power and the wealth that can flow from it.

Meanwhile, an entirely new type of what might once have been called an advertising or PR firm has now sprung up in what could loosely be called the disinformation industry. The Atlantic Council's Digital Forensic Research Lab identified a number of companies and individuals around the world who, for a fee, will spread lies and disinformation through social media and other venues on a highly targeted basis.

As Max Fisher wrote for the *New York Times*: "They sow discord, meddle in elections, seed false narratives and push viral conspiracies, mostly on social media. And they offer clients something precious: deniability."[25]

The first time this industry was outed in a big public way was in May 2021 when a company calling itself Fazze and claiming a nonexistent London address solicited a number of high-profile social media influencers to peddle lies about the Pfizer COVID-19 vaccine.

Researchers with the Atlantic Council found groups like this active in political campaigns in Europe and Africa as well as pushing anti-American memes in Iraq. They work for the Modi government in India, according to the *Times*, and push memes-for-hire for a variety of authoritarian regimes. It appears to be a variation on much of the anti–Hillary Clinton work that Cambridge Analytica had done for the Trump campaign in 2016.

Through trial and error, the industry is getting more and more sophisticated and effective. "The result," the *Times*' Fisher wrote, "is an accelerating rise in polarizing conspiracies, phony citizen groups and fabricated public sentiment, deteriorating our shared reality beyond even the depths of recent years."

Author Joshua Citerella described a new strategy to further confound our ability to know what's real and what isn't, which he dubbed the "slow red-pill," in his widely shared post on the donotresearch.net website.[26]

Across social media platforms, the people employing this strategy set up what look like the more common right-wing MAGA types of websites, using them to grow audiences of hundreds of thousands or millions of followers. When the site hits a critical and influential size, they drop in a hard-core racist or pro-violence meme.

There is instant blowback from many of the users, but the damage has been done—the viral message was delivered, and either the site deletes the offending post or the owner nukes the entire site to start elsewhere under a different name with the same strategy.[27]

Everybody, it seems, wants to ride the back of one Big Brother or another.

When Big Brother Trades Your Privacy for Its Own Power and Security

So, it's been a long day and you're feeling burned out—or it's been a great day and you want to party—so you go to the local pub for a drink and some friendly conversation. A stranger leans over and begins a conversation about your very favorite hobby or pastime, immediately drawing you in.

As you talk more, you start getting creeped out; this guy seems to know a lot about you, even though you've never met.

You try to back away from this stranger, but he gets in your face and tells you where you went to high school, what kinds of grades you had, what you do for a living, the names of people you work with, who your neighbors are, and all the dramas going on in your family. He has your email address and your credit score and knows lots of intimate details about where you've vacationed and with whom, and all about that night six years ago when you got particularly drunk and behaved in a way you prayed nobody would ever learn about.

The loss of privacy in America today is so profound that this scenario could play out if somebody simply saw your name on your credit card receipt for your drink and went to the bathroom for a few minutes with a smartphone and looked up your Facebook account and googled you.

It could also happen if he simply took your picture from across the room and tossed it to one of a growing number of companies offering facial recognition ability, with databases "scraped" from social media, including billions of individuals.

Similarly, think how you'd feel if when you walked into the pub and sat down to order a drink, the bartender told you that you'd have to leave because the camera over the front door had fed your picture to a facial recognition company that pinged him with information that you might be an undesirable or problematic customer.

Sound crazy? Rite Aid ran a program that did something similar to that, using facial recognition in more than 200 stores for eight years, but abandoned it when word leaked and the bad press began.[28]

Your face is just as unique as your fingerprint, Social Security number, or DNA, and we have extensive protections for all of those. Taking and processing a fingerprint or DNA sample is usually a complex, expensive, and time-consuming process, and stealing a Social Security number can require stealth and subterfuge.

On the other hand, scraping your photo at a busy restaurant off your Facebook page is easy and nearly instant; it takes a big computer a fraction of a millisecond, and the photo can be stored at little cost for as long as you live. And then it can be analyzed and the results transported to any customer anywhere in the world in the blink of an eye.

And it's already going on.

Clearview AI is a company that came out of a 2017 meeting of three Trump supporters, who had the audacious idea of scraping billions of pictures of people off of social media sites, particularly Facebook. They paired this ocean of data with a spiffy new facial recognition algorithm and seem to have produced a revolution in surveillance at scale.

While it was a violation of Facebook's terms of service, what they did wasn't illegal, and today they boast a collection of more than three billion people, complete with identities. Facebook, Venmo, Google, and LinkedIn sent them cease-and-desist letters in a classic closing-the-barn-door-after-the-horse-is-gone exercise.

It's also unlikely that it ever occurred to most of the Americans who posted pictures of themselves and their friends on social media in the decades leading up to now that their photos would be converted into digital "face prints" as unique as their fingerprints and that their face prints would live forever in the bowels of surveillance companies' and police departments' computers.

According to a 2021 report in the *New York Times*, the company, in its early days, "had made the app available to investors, potential investors and business partners, including a billionaire who used it to identify his daughter's date when the couple unexpectedly walked into a restaurant where he was dining."[29]

The app, according to public reporting, is now used by more than 3,000 law enforcement agencies, largely in the United States and in at least 27 countries.

Facial recognition isn't something new or exotic—if you have an Apple iPhone, you can use the technology built into your phone to identify and sort your own pictures. Facebook uses it to tag people and hook them together. It's become ubiquitous.

When 26 million Americans took to the streets in 2020 to protest the police murder of George Floyd, it's unlikely that many thought Attorney General William Barr's FBI and their own state governments would be using facial recognition to identify and build dossiers on each of them, but both the FBI and police have been doing exactly that since at least 2014, when the practice was first revealed by *The Intercept* and later confirmed by numerous media.[30,31,32]

Microsoft recently rolled out their product in this category, Microsoft Azure, which, their website said in June 2021, not only can identify people but "detect anger, contempt, disgust, fear, happiness, neutral, sadness, and surprise."[33]

A Russian company, NTechLab, rolled out an app like this called FindFace in 2016, making it available to regular users. "Within months of its release, it was reported that people were using the app to identify sex workers, porn stars and protesters." Facing bad publicity, the company pulled the product from public use; today it's installed in government-run surveillance cameras all over Moscow and other Russian cities.[34]

China is the world's leader in using facial recognition technology; it's become the foundation of their surveillance state, tracking the actions, behaviors, and emotions of over a billion people and assigning them each a "social credit score."

As then–Vice President Mike Pence said when visiting a conservative think tank in Washington, DC, in October 2018, quoting the Chinese government, "In the words of that program's official blueprint, it will 'allow the trustworthy to roam everywhere under heaven while making it hard for the discredited to take a single step.'"[35]

Local authorities in Suzhou, China, use the system to "name and shame people wearing their pajamas in public,"[36] but when directed toward the ethnic Uighur minority, it's used to determine who gets "reeducated" and who doesn't.[37]

Helen Davidson reported for *The Guardian* that while China says Uighurs are singled out for "vocational training," it's believed instead that their programs include "mass internment in camps, extensive technological and human surveillance, enforced labour programmes, enforced sterilisation of women and ideological 're-education.'"[38]

Back to the example that opened this chapter: even if you've deleted every single picture and story from your Facebook or other social media account—hell, even if you've deleted your *entire* Facebook account—the pictures have already been scraped, and besides that, Facebook has the ability to keep your information forever, even if it's not publicly visible, even if your account is closed.

"When you delete your account, all the user generated content is normally erased (although there are small exceptions)," Facebook's data disclosures say, "while all the log data is preserved—forever."

In addition, Facebook warns, "Keep in mind that information that others have shared about you is not part of your account and will not be deleted when you delete your account."[39]

Carol Davidsen, an Obama campaign official, gave a speech in 2015 that put a chilling codicil on Facebook's disclosures. "We were able to ingest the entire social network of the US on Facebook, which is most of the US," she told her audience. "The data is out there. You can't take it back. The Democrats have this information, so when they look at a voter file, they can say, 'Here are all the people they know.'"[40]

Of course, Republicans and Russians (among others) have that data too, and according to the Mueller investigation, they have already weaponized it against American voters. As Facebook itself revealed in 2017, at least 10 million Americans viewed pro-Trump or other political advertisements and content on Facebook that was paid for by Russians in the run-up to the 2016 election.[41]

In part 2, I wrote about the phenomenon of "social cooling"—the way people's behavior changes when they realize they're under surveillance. But how will our world and societies change when everybody *also* knows everything knowable about everybody else with a finger-flick on an app?

Are We Living with de Tocqueville's Kinder and Gentler Big Brother?

Reducing or even ending privacy is rarely an end in and of itself; it's a step toward a goal. That goal is usually a form of behavior modification, whether it's a government that wants its citizens to be more compliant or a company that wants to sell a product.

In that context, the loss of privacy we give up to Amazon, for example, in exchange for their being able to show us products that we probably would be interested in purchasing, is a trade-off most Americans are willing to make. Ditto for letting Google's Nest division control your thermostat and security cameras and know when you're home and when you're not, in exchange for increasing the general comfort and safety of your home.

Similarly, most Americans understand that companies that sell your personal data to banks, insurance companies, and potential landlords are just doing something similar to what the credit reporting industry does routinely, and we've tolerated that for generations.

But there's much bigger game at stake here.

Pretty much all the rules of all the games that we live by are defined by government.

Government decides which kinds of behavior are criminal and which are not.

Government decides how many years you'll go to jail for, say, possessing a marijuana cigarette or, if the hopes and dreams of today's GOP-controlled Texas Legislature come true, using birth control or seeking an abortion.

The rules of the game of business are also established by government. It's one of the reasons that companies spend billions of dollars a year lobbying federal and state governments to pass laws—rules of the game of business—that give them an unfair advantage relative to other companies and especially relative to their customers and the communities where they do business.

When it comes to who controls government, the stakes are incredibly high.

For example, President Richard Nixon changed the laws when he launched his War on Drugs in 1971, doing so in a way that he thought would let him more easily disrupt the anti-war and civil rights movements.

As Nixon's right-hand man John Ehrlichman told reporter Dan Baum, "We knew we couldn't make it illegal to be either against the war or Black, but by getting the public to associate the hippies with marijuana and Blacks with heroin and then criminalizing both heavily, we could disrupt those communities. We could arrest their leaders, raid their homes, break up their meetings, and vilify them night after night on the evening news. Did we know we were lying about the drugs? Of course we did."[42]

And when business controls government, they can postpone for decades things that might otherwise reduce their profits, like making it harder to purchase cigarettes or reducing the country's addiction to fossil fuels.

Government is also the only entity in modern society that has the legal right to deprive us of our freedom and even of our lives. Your employer can't put you in a cell and leave you there for years or hook you up to a lethal injection IV; government can and does do both.

Control of the Big Brother of government, thus, is the ultimate control.

In the United States, like other democracies, the government is chosen by the voters, which is where both the corporate and the governmental arms of Big Brother come in.

If you can control the behavior of the voters, whether you're Rupert Murdoch, Comcast, or a group with an ax to grind seeding Facebook, you can control the behavior of the government. And if you control the behavior of the government, you can rig the system to enhance your power and profits almost without limit.

This is where surveillance technology deployed on a massive scale by a small number of powerful companies, or surreptitiously by government, becomes so dangerous.

The Trump Era: A High-Water Mark of Big Brother Lies for Social Control

The tobacco, asbestos, and fossil fuel industries lied to us for decades, and those lies led to millions of deaths because they were successful in modifying the behavior of American consumers/voters. Similarly, most famously after 9/11, President George W. Bush and Vice President Dick Cheney were successful in lying us into two illegal and unnecessary wars, as President Lyndon Johnson had done before them in 1964 (Vietnam), President William McKinley did in 1898 (the Spanish-American War), and President James Polk did in 1846 (the Mexican-American War).

The plotline of George Orwell's famous novel *1984* was that the government of his hero, Winston, was lying about the threat that a foreign country represented, convincing citizens that they were at war when in fact there was no war and no threat. It really wasn't that different from what George W. Bush and Dick Cheney did in 2003, using the lie that the still-at-large Osama bin Laden was conspiring with Iraq's Saddam Hussein to again attack America.

All of those efforts, as grotesque as they were, were fairly public, as are most lobbying campaigns. Poisonous industries and poisonous politicians alike use what are essentially brute force techniques to influence or block legislation and start wars.

But things changed in a big way with the election of 2016, when a few billionaires teamed up (perhaps unwittingly) with Russia's President Putin to hand the American presidency to failed businessman and lifelong con artist Donald Trump.

Their main ammunition was Big Data, and the weapon that fired it was mostly Facebook, as has been so well documented by everybody from Robert Mueller and the FBI to Christopher Wylie, formerly of Cambridge Analytica, in his book *Mindf*ck* (see "Are We Doomed to Live Under Big Brother's Watchful Eye?" in part 4 for more on his book).

The Trump presidency represented a high-water mark for the white supremacist movement in the United States; they hadn't had a man who was openly one of their own in the White House since Woodrow Wilson, who screened *Birth of a Nation* in the White House and kicked off an American eugenics "racial purity" program that Hitler picked up (complete with US posters and slogans) and turned into his "final solution."

One Sunday night in June during the Trump-Biden election campaign of 2020 in the small Oregon town of Klamath Falls, about 200 locals showed up downtown with guns, baseball bats, and whatever other weapons they could find around the house to fight off the busloads of Black Antifa marauders whom Jewish billionaire George Soros had paid to get on buses in Portland and was sending their way.

Of course, Soros had done no such thing, and there were no busloads of Black people. But the warnings were all over the Klamath Falls Facebook group and, it turns out, similar Facebook groups for small towns all over America.

Literally, from coast to coast, white residents of small towns showed up in their downtown areas that weekend with guns, rifles, hammers, and axes prepared to do battle with busloads of Black people being sent into their small white towns by George Soros.

Nobody's sure to this day (other, probably, than Facebook) whether these messages, which activated frightened white people across the nation, came from local white supremacist groups trying to gauge what might happen if they actually could kick off a second American Civil War, or whether they came from a foreign government trying to tear America apart.

But they worked.

In the tiny town of Forks, Washington, frightened white people brought out chainsaws and cut down trees to block the road leading to their town. In South Bend, Indiana, police were overwhelmed by 911 calls from frightened white people wanting to know when the Antifa buses were arriving. And in rural Luzerne County, Pennsylvania, the local neighborhood internet group warned people that busloads of Black people were "organizing to riot and loot."

Similar stories played out from Danville, California, to Jacksonville, Florida, as documented by, among others, NBC News.[43]

Of course, it was all a fiction.

Reporters found that white people in these estimated-100-plus small towns almost universally didn't realize they'd been punked when the Antifa buses failed to arrive but instead thought that they had successfully kept them away by their menacing show of force. Many pledged to keep showing up night after night with their guns and hammers, thinking they were protecting their towns.[44]

The next day, a Monday, Fox News' Tucker Carlson took his swing at tearing America apart with a 25-minute rant arguing that Black Lives Matter had now essentially taken over America's news media and the white suburbs were next. "This may be a lot of things, this moment we're living through, but it is definitely not about black lives," Carlson gravely intoned. "Remember that when they come for you, and at this rate, they will."[45]

While Carlson didn't say who the "they" who will "come for you" were, or if they were Black people being sent by George Soros, the philanthropist has appeared for years as the puppet-master Jewish bogeyman on Fox News; on right-wing hate radio; and on anti-Semitic, racist, and Republican websites and Facebook groups.

The electoral strategy of frightening white people worked well for Richard Nixon in 1968 with his "Southern strategy" and for George H. W. Bush with his Willie Horton ad. It put them both in the White House.

After more than 240 years, however, we may finally be witnessing the birth pains of a transition into a newer and better America. Our media and our politics are both far more diverse than even in 2016, and after the disaster of the Trump presidency, the media have become more willing to call out lies by politicians.

History will tell if the final voice on this is that of hatemongers like Tucker Carlson, or if the simple demand of George Floyd's eulogist, Reverend Al Sharpton, that white supremacists "get your knee off our necks," will prevail here in the United States.

But for the moment, white supremacists and authoritarian Big Brother wannabes are still using the internet, social media generally, and Facebook particularly to promote and organize campaigns against minorities, democracy, and the US government itself. And it's not happening just here.

Beyond Elections: Big Brother in Social Media Can Kill

The same year that the Russian government, according to the FBI and the Mueller investigation, began an aggressive campaign seeding Facebook with pro-Trump and anti–Hillary Clinton propaganda and lies, the military of faraway Myanmar, formerly known as Burma, pulled together an estimated 700 information warfare specialists in a secret location.

The program had begun planning in 2012; workers had to surrender their own phones and computers and live totally in a government-controlled bubble as they drafted a series of lies and libels against the predominantly Muslim Rohingya minority.

Using photos of gruesome killings and other atrocities committed in other lands at other times but by Asian/Rohingya-looking people, they assembled a Big Lie that the

Rohingya were unrepentant Muslim terrorists committed to taking down the Myanmar government. After millions had seen the campaign, the government launched a Rwanda-style slaughter.

The Rohingya lived on land rich in natural resources, including valuable minerals, oil, and timber, and some of the nation's most productive farmland.[46] The military—and "Chinese,"[47] Korean,[48] Japanese,[49] and other multinational investors"— very much wanted that land, and in early 2016 the Myanmar military pulled the trigger on their operation, flooding Facebook with fake stories, fake news sites, and fake celebrity sites that were interspersed with the gruesome stories.[50]

Facebook is so widely used by that country's 18 million internet-connected citizens that most people there think it is the internet. The *New York Times* documented what happened next in an article titled "A Genocide Incited on Facebook, With Posts From Myanmar's Military."[51]

It led to what the *Times* called "murders,[52] rapes,[53] and the largest forced human migration in recent history."[54] It was an actual genocide, on a scale unseen in a generation, and it almost entirely levered off of Facebook.

As of this writing, the military leaders who put the genocide together are still in charge of the country and living large, buying weapons from Russia with money from Chinese and other multinational companies that are now developing the previously Rohingya regions.

Trump's attempt to take down American democracy with his rally and "march" on the US Capitol on January 6, 2021, was in large part similarly organized on private Facebook groups.

It failed, but if they had succeeded and politicians like Senators Ted Cruz, Tom Cotton, Josh Hawley, and Rick Scott had gotten their way and the election had been overturned and Trump installed as president for another four years, it's unlikely that you'd be reading this book right now.

As a progressive radio talk-show host with a substantial weekly audience, I'd probably be in prison , just as has happened in other countries (Hungary, Russia, Turkey, etc.) that were democracies for a while but flipped into authoritarianism. If you're an activist, if you'd shown up for BLM or other anti-racism or anti-Trump events—or even liked or shared their posts on social media—you might be occupying the jail cell next to me today.

This is real-world stuff with real-world consequences, and most Americans seem oblivious to how close we came to ending our 240-plus-years-long experiment in representative democracy. And so much of it was made possible by a few massive companies unrelentingly and secretly compiling extensive dossiers and digital profiles of every one of us.

PART FOUR

Putting the Reins on
Surveillance Capitalism

Software or Spyware?

The word processing program I'm using to write this book once mostly belonged to me (at least as long as I had the disc), but it no longer does.

As a lifelong writer, when the first version of Microsoft Word for DOS came out in 1983, I was an enthusiastic licensee. It came on a floppy disk, then the only delivery system available, and if you had the disk, you could run the program and even copy it to your hard drive and run it from there.

But, of course, disks could be copied, so over the years Microsoft evolved increasingly difficult systems to prevent copying disks, eventually migrating certification of license ownership onto and through the internet.

Initially, that didn't seem at all unreasonable. I'd pay for the latest version of the software, I'd install and authenticate it, and from there on I could use it without a problem.

Today it's quite different.

Microsoft now has my credit card number and charges me every year to renew my license; if I stop paying, the software becomes unusable. Which arguably isn't unreasonable, as I bought a license only to use it, and the terms of that license limited it to use during the period I paid for.

But now it's getting creepy.

There are features I can use in the program only if I make it entirely interactive with Microsoft's distant servers, via the internet. When I turn on these features, Word prompts me to save my documents with Microsoft OneDrive—on their servers. Where they (or any proficient hacker) can see everything I'm writing.

Do I really want Microsoft employees or hackers or spies for a dozen governments reading what I'm writing? Although I've not (yet) written anything illegal or particularly salacious, the idea offends my personal privacy sensibility. It's a little too close to Big Brother.

Of course, this is marketed as being "for my own convenience," so anywhere I may be, on any computer I may choose to use, I can access my files and the program. And there's truth to that on its face, although few realize the larger implications of Microsoft holding everything they've written.

This is not unique, by the way. The Firefox browser asks if I want to store my browsing activity and passwords with them, as does Apple, which offers their iCloud product to store everything on my computer and iPhone, from my pictures to my documents to my personal correspondence. Numerous celebrities took Apple up on this until hackers got into their accounts and embarrassing pictures started showing up on the web.

Now even "internet security" companies are pushing you to "back up" your data on their servers. At the studio, Norton constantly pesters me to put all my data on their servers, just like Apple and Microsoft do. Google, of course, probably already has it all or at least a good idea of what I'm writing, based on my search behaviors.

When I sign in to numerous social media sites, they ask if I will share my contacts with them; once they're given, it's impossible to ever get them back. The "convenience" is that the site will analyze your contacts and flag anybody in your address book who's also on the site. The downside is that people within these companies and hackers can now access your entire social, family, and business life with a few keystrokes.

I read around 20 books a year on my phone; it's convenient, and I can read at night without waking up Louise, as I don't need a reading light anymore.

But on a recent trip to Cuba, when I had no internet connection, I discovered that all my books—and all the information about which books I'd read, when, and what pages I'd left off reading on—were living on Apple's servers in California, and I'd have to wait until I was back in the United States to read the book I'd "bought" from Apple's online bookstore. Ditto for my Kindle books.

And it's not just social media, online books, and software. I bought a new Toyota plug-in hybrid Prius, and its "smart" features require me to create an account with Toyota to get software updates and access things like its maps/directions feature on the dashboard. There's even a LoJack-like system, where I can push a button above the dash and it triggers an emergency call . . . and if law enforcement wants, they can disable or otherwise seize control of my car at any time.

I have to admit that it's kind of cool being able to start my car remotely using an app via my Toyota account and get notifications on my smartphone when it's done charging.

Meanwhile, my car is sending gigabytes of data to Toyota about my driving habits, where and how I drive, what addresses I have stored in my address book, and how many miles I drive the car. Maybe it even tracks how many passengers I carry; there are certainly enough sensors in the car to make that possible.

With that data in hand, Toyota worked out a partnership with the Nationwide Insurance Company; if my driving patterns show that I'm a "good" driver, I can get a substantial discount on my car insurance. It's called the Toyota Insurance Management Solutions (TIMS) BrightDrive.

As their website says, "Your Toyota Is Smart Enough to Save You Money on Insurance! Connected Toyota drivers can enjoy a 10% discount right away and up to 40% at renewal."

And, of course, Toyota isn't unique in this.

A friend in West Virginia bought a new tractor, and it's the same deal. He has to register it with the manufacturer to get software updates, and now the company knows everything about how he uses it. And, presumably, they can sell that information to data brokers or companies that want to sell things to tractor owners like insurance or fertilizer or tractor attachments. Or maybe, knowing that he lives in a rural area, a sales pitch for a politician or to sign up for a new right-wing TV network.

While the justification for verifying the software licenses of users (including cars and tractors) is to verify who owns the license, the actual use of this system is vastly wider. It's used to collect information about you, how you use the product, and whom you know that may also be a potential customer. That information about you can then be a source of revenue for the Big Brother software licensor in a wide variety of ways, most of them relatively invisible to you.

And while companies say they're going to use your usage data to "improve their product" (just like when you call a company's sales or service line, their phone-tree system says, "Your call may be recorded to improve our service"), the reality is that they can just as easily offer a discount or rebate to a small selection of opt-in customers and derive the same kinds of feedback that way to improve their product.

Because there's virtually no regulation of these practices, they're metastasizing across product categories like kudzu in Georgia. The old joke used to be that if you're getting a free product on the internet (case in point, Facebook), then *you* are the product. But now it's even true of products for which we pay cold, hard cash.

Biometrics

You can change your address, phone number, email, and passwords. But you can never change your DNA, your finger-prints, or your face print.

For that reason, at the urging of the ACLU, back in 2008 Illinois passed the nation's first Biometric Information Privacy Act (BIPA). As of this writing, it still stands and is still unique among all the states; in every other state legislature, lobbyists for Big Tech have succeeded in blocking similar efforts.[1]

And with good reason. In 2015, 1.6 million Illinois residents who were also Facebook members sued the company in a class action for Facebook's photo tagging system, saying that it directly violated their rights to privacy under that state's BIPA. Confronting a near-certain conviction, Facebook settled out of court in February 2021 for $650 million and changed the way their system works.[2]

Illinois' law explicitly requires companies that collect or store biometric data (fingerprints, DNA, retina or iris scans, voiceprints, hand scans, and "other unique biological informa-tion") to inform in writing each person from whom such data is collected of the purpose and length of time for which the data is stored and how it will be used.

They must also, after informing the person that their biometric data is being harvested, explicitly ask for the person's consent. This includes everything from computers and smartphones that automatically unlock in response to a fingerprint or face scan to companies that collect DNA for genealogy or medical purposes.

There's good cause for concern.

In January 2020, Robert Julian-Borchak Williams, a Black Detroit resident, pulled into his driveway the day before his 42nd birthday, only to have his car blocked in by a police car. Two cops jumped out and handcuffed and arrested Williams in front of his freaked-out wife and two young daughters.

When he and his wife asked the police why a law-abiding family man with a full-time job was being arrested, they refused to answer, instead showing Williams and his wife a felony warrant for an unspecified "larceny." He was hauled off to the police station, booked, and searched; had his fingerprints, DNA, and mug shot taken; and was thrown into a cell.

The next day, when he was finally interrogated, he learned that he was charged with shoplifting $3,800 worth of high-end watches from a Detroit Shinola store two years earlier. The store's surveillance system had caught a Black man who was about the same general size and weight of Williams in the act, and the store had recently hired a "loss prevention" company to review years of security camera footage.

The company handed the photo off to Detroit police, who ran it through a commercial facial recognition company's database; Williams's face, presumably scraped from Facebook and other social media accounts (he'd never been arrested), came up.

It wasn't Williams who'd stolen the watches, but that arrest not only rattled him and his family, it also broke his four-year streak of never missing a day of work. When he bailed himself out of jail, lawyers who assumed he was guilty quoted him $7,000 and up to defend him, and he nearly lost his job.

As Kashmir Hill wrote for the *New York Times*, "Mr. Williams and his wife have not talked to their neighbors about what happened. They wonder whether they need to put their daughters into therapy. Mr. Williams's boss advised him not to tell anyone at work."[3]

When the arrest—the first in the nation based on an incorrect face print—hit the media, Senators Jeff Merkley (D-Oregon) and Ed Markey (D-Massachusetts) and Representatives Pramila Jayapal (D-Washington), Ayanna Pressley (D-Massachusetts), Rashida Tlaib (D-Michigan), and Katherine Clark (D-Massachusetts) introduced the Facial Recognition and Biometric Technology Moratorium Act in both houses of Congress.[4]

A few months before Williams's story was published in the *Times*, Merkley and Senator Cory Booker (D-New Jersey) had introduced the Ethical Use of Facial Recognition Act, explicitly designed to safeguard Americans' right to privacy by instituting a moratorium on all federal governmental use of the technology until Congress passed legislation outlining specific uses for the data.[5]

More recently, Merkley and Senator Bernie Sanders (I-Vermont) introduced the National Biometric Information Privacy Act of 2020, based on the 2008 law in Illinois. The Act requires businesses to get your opt-in consent before collecting or sharing your biometrics, to delete your biometrics in a timely fashion, and to store your biometrics securely, as well as empowering Americans to sue businesses that break the rules.

Now that the lobbying muscle (and dollars) of Big Tech exceeds that of Big Oil and Big Tobacco, it's going to take a loud outcry from people for these proposals to ever become law.

Step one would be getting money out of politics, which is the subject of two other books in this series (*The Hidden History of American Oligarchy* and *The Hidden History of the War on Voting*).

The "Right to Be Forgotten"

In 2013, a Spaniard named Mario Costeja González searched his own name on Google. He discovered a newspaper story about the forced sale of a property he had owned in 1998, with the proceeds of that sale going to satisfy the Spanish tax collector. González had long ago put that year's economic troubles behind him and was both embarrassed and outraged to see the link come up over and over when his name was searched.[6]

He sued Google, claiming, essentially, that he had a right to be forgotten, and when he won the case in May 2014, it really got the European Union (EU) privacy ball rolling.

The EU now has a set of laws regulating how much of your data can be collected by Big Tech and under what circumstances, how it can be used, and your right to have it deleted. It's called the General Data Protection Regulation (GDPR), and there's a website devoted to it: gdpr.eu.[7]

The GDPR website says the following:

The General Data Protection Regulation (GDPR) is the toughest privacy and security law in the world. Though it was drafted and passed by the European Union (EU), it imposes obligations onto organizations anywhere, so long as they target or collect data related to people in the EU. The regulation was put into effect on May 25, 2018. The GDPR will levy harsh fines against those who violate its privacy and security standards, with penalties reaching into the tens of millions of euros.[8]

You may have noticed that starting a few years ago, websites began to ask your permission to track you or store cookies on your computer; that's to comply with GDPR rules.

The EU first tried to address internet privacy in a big way in 2012 with a series of conferences and white papers on various aspects of the issue. Most were grounded in Articles 7 and 8 of the Charter of Fundamental Rights of the European Union, which was drafted in 2000 and took legal effect in 2009.[9,10]

Article 7 references the right of all European Union citizens to have their private and family lives "respected," and Article 8 lays out citizens' right to their own personal data.

The GDPR is now vigorously enforced. When a half million booking details of British Airways passengers were hacked, the EU hit that company with a $230 million fine. Marriott lost data to hackers on 339 million guests because it hadn't updated an old system and paid a $123 million fine; and just on the hidden data that it was collecting on Android phone users, Google paid a $57 million fine.[11]

Under these rules, you're entitled to know the details of how your data is collected and used, to know what data has been collected (at no cost to you for finding out), to have any mistakes in your data corrected, to have your data deleted under reasonable circumstances, and to refuse to hand over data that you consider personal.[12]

While there have been numerous attempts to put this into US law at both the federal and state levels, the most high profile was a "right to be forgotten" bill introduced in the New York State Assembly and Senate in 2017, AB 5323 and S05287. It would have given companies 30 days from a "request from an individual" to pull data off the internet when it met certain criteria.

Language from the legislation included the following:

- [A]ll search engines and online speakers shall remove . . . content about such individual, and links or indexes to any of the same, that is "inaccurate," "irrelevant," "inadequate," or "excessive,"

- and without replacing such removed . . . content with any disclaimer [or] takedown notice.

- "[I]naccurate," "irrelevant," "inadequate," or "excessive" shall mean content . . . which after a significant lapse in time from its first publication . . . is no longer material to current public debate or discourse,

- especially when considered in light of the financial, reputational and/or demonstrable other harm that the information . . . is causing to the requester's professional, financial, reputational or other interest,

- with the exception of content related to convicted felonies, legal matters relating to violence, or a matter that is of significant current public interest, and as to which the requester's role with regard to the matter is central and substantial.[13]

The legislation, which imposed damages of $250 per day plus lawyers' fees, was defeated by politicians in the pockets of Big Tech before even coming up for a vote.

In June 2019, the Pew Research Center conducted a poll of Americans on these issues, particularly the right to "keep things about themselves from being searchable online." The other side of the question was whether it was more important to be able to "discover potentially useful information about others."

Americans, 74 to 23 percent, preferred the right to keep things private from both government and commercial Big Brother entities or even to be forgotten.[14]

YouTube, Facebook, and Porn: Regulate Social Media

While the field of research into the way social media may cause political radicalization is fairly new, serious scientific examinations of how watching porn can alter behavior go back decades. Turns out, they're pretty much the same.

While much of the research, particularly that suggesting that porn viewing leads to antisocial behavior out in the world, is controversial and still the subject of scientific debate,[15] one finding is relatively uncontroversial: that over time, many heavy users of porn will seek out more and more extreme content to get the same satisfaction.[16]

As Norman Doidge wrote in his 2007 book *The Brain That Changes Itself*, "When pornographers boast that they are pushing the envelope by introducing new, harder themes, what they don't say is that they must, because their customers are building up a tolerance to the content."[17]

Humans are novelty-seeking machines. Give us a little buzz—be it with a shot of heroin or cocaine, or an exhilarating new experience—and curiosity can quickly become a craving. Over time, it takes more and more to give us the same buzz, a process that we generally liken to addiction but applies to all sorts of things, from snack foods to violence in video games and movies to opioids.

In every case, the neurochemical process that draws us initially to these things—novelty-seeking behavior mediated by bursts of "happy chemicals" like dopamine in the brain—is the same: a system originally wired into our hunter-gatherer brains to increase our chances of survival.

The excitement of the hunt—as much as our hunger—drew us out into the dangerous world of jungle, forest, or savannah to find food. And highly concentrated nutrients—like a tree full of honey—gave us an even bigger buzz, guaranteeing we'd search for more.

It's also how social media works, and the social media companies know it.

A 2014 study titled *Down the (White) Rabbit Hole: The Extreme Right and Online Recommender Systems* found, "A process is observable whereby users accessing an ER [Extreme Rightwing] YouTube video are likely to be recommended further ER content, leading to immersion in an ideological bubble in just a few short clicks."[18]

Real-world confirmation was easy for Zeynep Tufekci, a reporter who chronicled her experience in the *New York Times*. Noting that she didn't normally watch right-wing extremist content on YouTube, she said that she needed to confirm a few Trump quotes during the 2016 election, so she watched several of his speeches on that site.

"Soon I noticed something peculiar," Tufekci wrote. "YouTube started to recommend and 'autoplay' videos for me that featured white supremacist rants, Holocaust denials, and other disturbing content."

Curious, she created a few new YouTube accounts and began looking at videos on subjects from Hillary Clinton to Bernie Sanders to seemingly nonpolitical topics like vegetarianism.

Right across the board, she found that "videos on vegetarianism led to videos on veganism" and "videos about jogging led to videos about running ultramarathons." YouTube just kept cranking up the ante, feeding her Hillary and Bernie watching into conspiracy screeds about 9/11 and other worries of the extreme left.

"It seems as if you are never 'hard core' enough for YouTube's recommendation algorithm," she wrote. "It promotes, recommends and disseminates videos in a manner that appears to constantly up the stakes. Given its billion or so users, YouTube may be one of the most powerful radicalizing instruments of the 21st century."[19]

Algorithms put together by other social media platforms appear to do the same thing (they're all proprietary, need-to-know trade secrets and not available for oversight even to government agencies). The fairly well-known example is Facebook's algorithm leading users to such radical content that they would end up voting for Donald Trump and then invade the US Capitol and seriously injure more than 130 police officers, many ending up in the hospital.[20]

In every case, the algorithm's goal is to "increase engagement" so that the social media company can sell more ads at a higher price.

Facebook's algorithm even placed paid ads for weapons next to content filled with inflammatory lies and misinformation about the November 2020 election, a fact that wasn't lost on 23 members of Congress who grilled Facebook CEO Mark Zuckerberg about it in early 2021.[21]

As a society, we generally try to regulate things that provoke this kind of brain-seizing response.

Pharmaceuticals and alcohol are tightly regulated, as is gambling, because addiction to them has dire societal consequences. We mandated warnings on cigarettes and food products so that people can understand the threats and consequences. And we regulate sex and violence in mainstream media.

When Congress discovered that processed food manufacturers were using research on addiction responses to determine how much salt, sugar, and fat to put into their products to produce repeated and increasing consumption—leading to a nationwide obesity crisis—they mandated transparency. Food labels now disclose the content of processed food products, including the amount of each of these "addictive" substances.

A good start toward regulating Big Brother social media companies would be to do the same: require them to publish their algorithms, both in source code and with a plain English explanation, so that at the very least we can learn *how* we're being manipulated and radicalized.

How Much Big Brother Will Modern People Tolerate?

Ben Franklin is often quoted as having said, "Those who would give up essential Liberty, to purchase a little temporary Safety, deserve neither Liberty nor Safety." Privacy advocates often cite it as if privacy or freedom were the topic of Franklin's quote, but it was really a speech he wrote for the Pennsylvania General Assembly during the French and Indian War (1754–1763) two decades before America became independent of Great Britain.

The legislature had just passed a tax on the massive landholdings of the Penn family, who were vigorously lobbying the governor to veto the property tax. Instead, the Penns suggested, they'd give a onetime gift of cash to the state for it to protect itself for a period of a few years ("a little temporary safety") but did *not* want the state to put a perpetual, year-after-year tax on the books.

Franklin knew that Pennsylvania needed the funds to protect itself from both the French *and* the Indians, so the "liberty" he was talking about was the ability of that state's government to raise taxes to provide itself with "safety." The mind-bogglingly wealthy Penn family was hindering that liberty by messing with the political process, what today we'd call lobbying.[22]

Far from being about privacy or freedom, it was really an early statement against letting rich people buy, own, or influence politicians.

That said, Franklin's quote fits into the context of this book even better than the simplistic idea that he was speaking about keeping corporations or government out of our business. It raises the issue of safety/security and whose interest government serves.

Do you feel safe walking down the street at night? Does government protect you from predation, or is government the predator itself? And if government is limiting liberty, on whose behalf is it doing so?

Back in the 1990s, I published a book positing that ADHD wasn't a brain disease but instead was an adaptive neurological difference that served our hunter-gatherer ancestors well but disadvantaged people living in agricultural-industrial societies. *Time* magazine published an article about the book, and it exploded in both sales and influence—by the 2000s the educational and psychological communities (and parent groups) were abuzz about my "Hunter in a Farmer's World" hypothesis.

I spent years traveling around the world speaking to groups ranging from parents' organizations to school boards to conventions of psychologists and psychiatrists. Thus, a wealthy parents' group in Singapore invited me to talk with them about ways their schools could become more ADHD-friendly.

Coming in from the airport, I marveled at how beautiful and well maintained the city was. There was no trash, everybody was well-dressed and bustling about, and the city's buildings were elegant and modern. Top-notch. Five-star. There wasn't even any sign of gum stains on the sidewalks. The cab driver kept slowing down whenever his car bumped above a particular speed (my recollection was that it was 50 mph) because a little bell would ring from below the dash. He explained to me that it was to prevent him from endangering anybody by speeding. I didn't realize at the time the considerable legal peril he faced for breaking even the most minor of Singapore's laws.

The parents' group put me up in one of the top business hotels in the city-state; it was grand, elegant, stately, and modern. My hosts picked me up for my talk and took me to the venue, where I gave an hourlong presentation followed by a Q&A session.

Toward the end, one of the parents asked, "How can we put these changes you suggest into place in our schools? They seem very resistant to change."

I answered that they should contact their politicians, pointing out that in democracies most real and meaningful structural changes in government institutions like public schools usually came about through a political process. The room was strangely silent for a long moment, and then one of my hosts stood up, thanked me, and wrapped up the event.

Over a meal after the presentation, I asked my hosts (a half-dozen of the parents who were leaders of the parents' group) what they thought of the presentation and if they had any thoughts or suggestions for changes I could make for future presentations elsewhere. One said, somewhat shyly, "I'd suggest you may want to reconsider discussing politics in the context of education."

I was baffled but let it pass, and our conversation moved along. It was a long, wonderful multicourse meal, and about three hours later I was dropped off at my hotel.

Walking into my room, I was shocked. Every drawer had been opened and things were on the floor. The mattress had been lifted off the bed. My suitcase had been opened and its contents spilled all over the floor, and some of my clothes in the closet were moved around as if they had been searched.

I called hotel security to report what I thought was a break-in or robbery, although I couldn't immediately see that anything was missing. The head of security showed up in my room five minutes later with the hotel manager. They looked around the room with no shock or alarm.

And then the manager said, with a hint (but only a hint) of apology in his voice, "The police were here," as if that explained everything.

"They did this?" I asked, as I recall.

He nodded and said, "Presumably."

"Why?" I demanded.

Both men shrugged. The head of security asked me if I'd engaged in anything illegal while in Singapore, particularly bringing illegal drugs into the country, and I indignantly denied even the possibility. They shrugged again and offered to send a maid up to help put the room back together.

The next morning, I was set to fly on to Germany, and one of the couples who attended my speech had promised to join me at the hotel for breakfast. Over the meal, I explained what had happened with a fair amount of outrage. They simply listened and nodded.

When I finished my rant, wondering out loud if cops in Singapore ran robbery operations with impunity and just hadn't found anything worth stealing in my stuff, one of them said, "I'm sorry to hear that happened. It's what I was concerned about when I heard you mention politics."

I was astonished; while they wouldn't say it out loud, the implication was clear that the police had torn my room apart because I'd mentioned politics and that such things were not uncommon in Singapore.

"They were trying to send me a message?" I asked.

"And us," one said, looking about to see if anybody was listening to our conversation. They then changed the topic, clearly uncomfortable even talking about the consequences of speaking about politics.

In the two decades since my adventure there, Singapore has loosened up considerably but could still be described in some ways as a police state. And the business community loves it. Capitalism, after all, does not need a liberal democracy to survive; witness the success of authoritarian communist China.

A union, for example, is literally democracy in the workplace. Workers elect their own leaders and vote on their own requests and demands of management. When Amazon crushed a unionization effort at an Alabama facility in 2021, it wasn't because the company liked or hated democracy; they just didn't want workers to have the ability to reduce the company's profits by demanding a tiny slice of them as compensation.

For that matter, Amazon's practices of connecting millions of Americans' Ring doorbells to each other and to local police, or making the default setting on their Alexa/Echo products that your internet connection is now shared with your neighbors or anybody who happens to drive by, aren't about creating a fascist police state. They're just trying—and doing a damned good job of it—to provide seamless *security* for their customers, thus increasing their market share and bottom line.

But what if the neofascist Republican dream of an authoritarian oligarchic state happens here in full? What if your own doorbell, thermostat, and internet radio gizmo all become instruments of state "security," and police are now using Amazon's Rekognition brand of facial recognition to see who comes and goes to your home, looking for dissidents? How can you escape when the smart speaker in your home is funneling any subversive conversations you have straight to the FBI?

Corporations, almost by definition, are generally democracy-neutral. As German industrialist Fritz Thyssen's apologia autobiography *I Paid Hitler* points out, one of the core elements of 20th-century fascism was the *merger* of state and corporate interests.[23]

Vice President Henry Wallace wrote about this in an op-ed for the *New York Times* on April 9, 1944, at the height of the war against the Axis powers of Germany and Japan:

> *The really dangerous American Fascists are not those who are hooked up directly or indirectly with the Axis. The FBI has its finger on those.*
>
> *The dangerous American Fascist is the man who wants to do in the United States in an American way what Hitler did in Germany in a Prussian way. The American Fascist would prefer not to use violence. His method is to poison the channels of public information. With a Fascist the problem*

*is never how best to present the truth to the public but how
best to use the news to deceive the public into giving the Fascist and his group more money or more power.*

Wallace bluntly laid out his concern about the same happening here in America:

*If we define an American Fascist as one who in case of
conflict puts money and power ahead of human beings,
then there are undoubtedly several million Fascists in
the United States. There are probably several hundred
thousand if we narrow the definition to include only those
who in their search for money and power are ruthless and
deceitful. . . . They are patriotic in time of war because it
is to their interest to be so, but in time of peace they follow
power and the dollar wherever they may lead.*[24]

Americans once believed we had guardrails to prevent our
nation from becoming like Singapore. Donald Trump proved
they weren't as robust as we thought.

And now, as the key elements of a corporate-police state are
being constructed all around us, it's more important than ever
to take stock of Big Brother and get his most dangerous potential actions under control.

The Fourth Amendment Is
Not for Sale Act of 2021

Government agencies are generally forbidden by law from
spying on residents of the United States (there is some
nuance, depending on citizenship) without a warrant, but not

only are there no laws preventing such spying by Big Tech—it's actually at the core of their business model. As described earlier, there's a multibillion-dollar industry engaged in collecting, compiling, collating, and reselling information about the most intimate details of your and my lives, from how and when we eat and sleep, and where we go, to how often and how vigorously we have sex. And, of course, who we're interacting with and the general or implied content of those meetings and conversations.

While it's illegal for government to collect and compile such information without a court's oversight, both the Electronic Communications Privacy Act of 1986 and the Foreign Intelligence Surveillance Act of 1978, and dozens of others, carry a loophole that government can drive a truckload of data through—and routinely does. The laws forbid government from collecting that information—from spying on us—but there's virtually nothing in any of these and other laws that prevents the government from simply *buying* that information from the for-profit companies that make it their business to spy on us.

And buy it they do. Police agencies around the country buy access to databases of personal information ranging from when and where we are and who we're with to our face prints, DNA, and other highly unique and personal data. Local police agencies and US Immigration and Customs Enforcement (ICE) are apparently the most aggressive purchasers and users of this type of data, although nobody's really sure because of government secrecy.

In early 2021, Senator Ron Wyden of Oregon led 20 other senators of both parties in introducing the Fourth Amendment

Is Not for Sale Act,[25] which was simultaneously brought in the House, led by Representatives Jerry Nadler (D-New York) and Zoe Lofgren (D-California). Shortly after, Big Tech and Big Data began the lobbying blitz. Keep an eye on this and similar legislation.

Are We Doomed to Live under Big Brother's Watchful Eye?

China's new "social credit system" is a dystopian warning of what America needs to absolutely avoid as we head deeper into the 21st century, particularly after our brush with Trumpian authoritarian rule. In these regards, Big Brother could become a true enemy of democracy.

That system, implemented through government collaboration with a group of the largest social media, banking, and online commerce sites in the country (among others), scores individual Chinese citizens based on a whole spectrum of criteria, from how promptly they pay their taxes and bills, to "offensive" speech in public or online, to individual behaviors like driving erratically, jaywalking, playing loud music on public transit, not showing up for restaurant or hotel reservations, or smoking in nonsmoking areas.[26]

WeChat (owned by tech giant Tencent, with over a billion registered users), China's equivalent of Facebook, compiles much of the social information used, while Weibo, China's version of Twitter, feeds the government data about individuals who've posted flagged content, as well as directly censoring individuals who are socially "disruptive."[27]

Alipay (owned by tech/banking giant Alibaba), China's version of PayPal, tracks both financial transactions and banking activity, helping create—along with a few other banking giants—financial credit trustworthiness scores that also become part of the government's social credit system.[28]

Taobao (also owned by Alibaba), China's version of Amazon, with sales of up to $10 billion *a day*, knows everything you've ever ordered online or even browsed and thus can profile your lifestyle in a way that could also affect your social credit system score.[29]

People who score poorly can lose their ability to travel (China blocked 29 million air tickets and six million high-speed-rail tickets in 2019 based on these scores), become unable to book a restaurant or hotel reservation, have their internet slowed down, and even lose the ability to get high-status jobs or enroll their children in prestigious private schools or universities.[30]

A high social credit score gets you better and faster reservations, preferred access to schools, shorter waits at hospitals and doctors' offices, discounts across a broad range of products and services, and better employment offers.[31]

The core idea of China's social credit system is, they say, "If trust is broken in one place [by one individual], restrictions are imposed [on that individual] everywhere."[32]

Also feeding the entire system is the world's largest network of surveillance cameras with facial recognition, capable of determining not only a person's identity but also their emotional state, giving China a continuous record of everybody's whereabouts and behavior.[33]

People with low social scores find themselves blocked from a whole range of activities, from flying to banking to renting to online matchmaking services for singles.[34] Their faces can show up online, on billboards, and even as "wall of shame" types of outings in theaters prior to movie showings. As the Chinese government declared in a 2014 document, "keeping trust is glorious and breaking trust is disgraceful."[35]

They can redeem themselves—typically a process that takes two to five years—by participating in remedies ranging from being fiscally responsible, to giving blood and volunteering for social activities, to praising the government on social media (among other things).[36]

While America, at the level of government, is not yet close to anything like this, the bits and pieces of it are scattered all around our corporate landscape.

Credit scores haven't yet incorporated things like speeding tickets or patronizing drinking establishments, but insurance companies are buying and selling that information and using it to set rates.

Companies haven't gotten totally punitive against activists, but I remember a time when I'd trash-talked Facebook's role in Trump's election on my radio show during that administration, and—perhaps coincidentally—my personal Facebook account was nuked by the company without explanation.

After sending them my driver's license multiple times, I still didn't have access to the main way I kept in contact with my three brothers and their kids and families back in Michigan, not to mention old friends and more distant relatives. After several months, I wrote an op-ed about the experience that was widely circulated, and my account suddenly appeared back online.

Christopher Wylie, formerly of Cambridge Analytica, wrote about a similar but far more draconian experience in 2018 when American and British media revealed that he was going to testify to Congress and federal authorities about how that company had used Facebook to help get Donald Trump elected president. "The ban was nothing more than a dick move by Facebook," he wrote in his book *Mindf*ck*.

His experience was considerably more drastic than mine, however (and I still can't say that mine wasn't just an error).

"The company [Facebook] demanded," he wrote, "that I hand over my phone and personal computer and said that the only way for me to be reinstated was, in effect, to give them the same information I was providing the authorities. Facebook behaved as if it were a nation-state, rather than a company."[37]

Then there's the story of a game developer who woke up one day to find that Google had not only deleted his Gmail account with all his history and contacts but also signed him out of the Android operating system he used for his phone and tablet, rendering them useless. Every effort to reach the company or even get an explanation, according to reporting in *Business Insider*, was futile.[38]

Something similar happened to the husband of a software engineer who goes by the Twitter handle @miguelytob, and as of this writing, his story is still live on that platform, including screen shots.[39]

Such bans also happen to people on the right: Donald Trump and many of his allies have famously been banned from Twitter, and if you'd searched (as I did) online in May 2021 for "China social credit score America," you'd have gotten literally thousands of hits from right-wing websites that had been banned from YouTube, had their banking accounts frozen, or lost their ability to post on other social media.

One site that hits high in the search results belongs to the founder of the right-wing social media site Gab, and another has a big banner at the top that said in June of 2021: "ALERT: On October 15, 2020 YouTube terminated BOTH [of our] YouTube channels without warning or cause. On October 22, 2020 Patreon terminated [our] Patreon page without warning or cause. This is economic warfare friends."[40]

For most Americans, it's easy to dismiss the experiences of conspiracy-nut or right-wing commentators and websites and a former president, who were all fascism-friendly; I'm frankly not sorry to see Trump banned from Twitter, for example. It's almost certainly better for our democracy.

But these are examples of real social and political power held by private corporations, and America should have a public conversation about how that power is acquired, held, and used; by whom; and with what oversight and controls.

China is using a communist-capitalist model and is openly, nakedly repressive. The more old-fashioned version, pioneered by Benito Mussolini in the 1920s, is called *fascism* and involves merging state and corporate functions.

American governments routinely outsource functions they want to remain secret because corporations don't have the transparency and accountability requirements we've built into government. The George W. Bush administration's outsourcing of torture to companies like Blackwater is one of the more famous examples that, had there not been a few leakers and whistleblowers, we'd probably never know anything about.

The infrastructure for a repressive state is largely in place in America; after all, much of the technology that the Chinese are using was developed here, and what they're doing that's home-grown, America can simply buy from them.

We're partway down a dangerous road, in terms of both corporate and government Big Brothers, in ways that are incompatible with democracy. Most Americans are blissfully unaware of either of these attacks on our privacy and, ultimately, our democracy, and of the new way these technological changes will alter how the world will fight future wars.

The qualified good news is that politicians on both sides of the aisle are becoming progressively more and more sensitive to the issues (even if sometimes for very different reasons). Without an outraged, mobilized, and engaged citizenry, we are, at this moment, heading down the road toward a China- or Singapore-style form of authoritarian government and corporatized surveillance economy that is fundamentally incompatible with our founding principles.

NOTES

Introduction: The Big Picture of Social Control vs. Democracy

1. Anthony Summers, *Official and Confidential: The Secret Life of J. Edgar Hoover* (New York: Putnam, 1993).

2. https://www.washingtonpost.com/entertainment/white-supremacy -hollywood-villains/2021/01/15/515f5386-5696-11eb-a08b -f1381ef3d207_story.html

3. https://www.nytimes.com/2014/11/16/magazine/what-an -uncensored-letter-to-mlk-reveals.html?_r=1

4. Lamar Waldron and I investigated this and other aspects of the John F. Kennedy and Robert F. Kennedy assassinations for over a decade. Our reporting is compiled in our book *Legacy of Secrecy: The Long Shadow of the JFK Assassination*, by Lamar Waldron with Thom Hartmann (New York: Counterpoint Books, 2013).

5. https://www.thedailybeast.com/cambridge-analyticas-real-role-in -trumps-dark-facebook-campaign

6. https://www.thedailybeast.com/zuckerberg-maybe-im-in-cambridge -analyticas-files

7. https://www.fastcompany.com/90420833/ex-cambridge-analytica -employee-if-trump-wins-in-2020-blame-facebook

8. https://www.wired.com/2016/11/facebook-won-trump-election-not -just-fake-news/

9. https://www.washingtonpost.com/technology/2020/09/28/trump -2016-cambridge-analytica-suppression/

10. https://www.nytimes.com/2016/11/21/us/many-in-milwaukee -neighborhood-didnt-vote-and-dont-regret-it.html

11. https://madison.com/ct/news/local/govt-and-politics/election -matters/why-did-wisconsin-see-its-lowest-presidential-election-voter -turnout-in-20-years/article_6dd2887f-e1fc-5ed8-a454-284d37204669 .html

12. https://www.nytimes.com/2020/01/07/technology/facebook -andrew-bosworth-memo.html

13. This and multiple other Rusticus quotes are in my book *Unequal Protection*, most quoted from the account of the Boston Tea Party by George Robert Twelves Hughes, *A Retrospect of the Boston Tea-Party, With a Memoir of George R. T. Hewes, a Survivor of the Little Band of Patriots Who Drowned the Tea in Boston Harbour in 1773*.

14. https://www.nytimes.com/2018/10/15/technology/myanmar -facebook-genocide.html

Part One: Big Brother and Social Control

1. Benjamin Franklin, *The Complete Works in Philosophy, Politics, and Morals of the Late Dr. Benjamin Franklin, Now First Collected and Arranged: With Memoirs of His Early Life* (Farmington Hills, MI: Gale-Sabin Americana, 2012; originally published 1806).
2. Joseph Priestley, *A General History of the Christian Church, to the Fall of the Western Empire* (1803), https://www.google.com/books/edition/_/WD6jDJMfaeYC?hl=en&gbpv=1.
3. https://www.hallvworthington.com/Persecutions/Part-6.html
4. https://www.dover.nh.gov/government/city-operations/library/history/the-whipping-of-the-quaker-women.html
5. Ibid.
6. http://homepages.rootsweb.com/~ahopkins/southwick/church_history.htm
7. Franklin, *The Complete Works, in Philosophy, Politics, and Morals, of the Late Dr. Benjamin Franklin.*
8. Daniel Quinn, *Ishmael* (New York: Bantam Books, 2017).
9. Peter Farb, *Man's Rise to Civilization as Shown by the Indians of North America from Primeval Times to the Coming of the Industrial State* (New York: E. P. Dutton, 1968).
10. Aristotle, *Politics*, trans. Benjamin Jowett, written 350 BCE, http://classics.mit.edu/Aristotle/politics.1.one.html.
11. Ephesians 6:5.
12. Edmund S. Morgan, *American Slavery, American Freedom* (New York: W. W. Norton & Co., 2003).
13. Noel Ignatiev, *How the Irish Became White* (New York: Routledge, 1995).
14. Ian Haney López, *White by Law: The Legal Construction of Race*, Revised and Updated 10th Anniversary Edition (New York: New York University Press, 2006).
15. Peggy McIntosh, "White Privilege: Unpacking the Invisible Knapsack," *Peace and Freedom Magazine*, July/August 1989, 10–12.
16. https://shec.ashp.cuny.edu/exhibits/show/slavecommunities/item/863
17. New Hampshire outlawed slavery in 1777, with a total population of about 100 African slaves in the state at the time.
18. Patrick Rael, "The Distinction Between Slavery and Race in U.S. History," *Black Perspectives*, November 27, 2016, https://www.aaihs.org/the-distinction-between-slavery-and-race-in-u-s-history/.

19. Frederick Douglass, *The Life and Times of Frederick Douglass* (Boston, MA: De Wolfe & Fiske Co., 1892).

20. https://www.law.cornell.edu/constitution/fourth_amendment

21. https://avalon.law.yale.edu/18th_century/fed69.asp

22. https://www.farmersalmanac.com/thomas-crapper-story-31372

23. https://supreme.justia.com/cases/federal/us/367/497/

24. https://supreme.justia.com/cases/federal/us/277/438/

25. Ibid.

26. https://supreme.justia.com/cases/federal/us/381/479/

27. Ibid.

28. https://supreme.justia.com/cases/federal/us/389/347/

29. https://www.ftc.gov/enforcement/statutes/fair-credit-reporting-act

30. https://www.justice.gov/opcl/privacy-act-1974

31. https://www.ftc.gov/enforcement/rules/rulemaking-regulatory-reform-proceedings/childrens-online-privacy-protection-rule

32. https://corporate.findlaw.com/finance/congress-passes-financial-services-modernization-act-of-1999.html

33. https://www.theguardian.com/world/2013/jun/06/nsa-phone-records-verizon-court-order

34. https://www.theguardian.com/world/2013/jun/06/us-tech-giants-nsa-data

35. https://www.washingtonpost.com/graphics/politics/usa-freedom-act/

36. *The Lives of Others (Das Leben der Anderen)*, 2006, https://www.imdb.com/title/tt0405094/.

37. https://www.britannica.com/topic/Stasi

38. https://theintercept.com/2021/05/03/car-surveillance-berla-msab-cbp/

39. https://www.politico.com/newsletters/morning-cybersecurity/2019/09/12/israel-blamed-for-dc-stingrays-738932

40. https://www.aclu.org/issues/privacy-technology/surveillance-technologies/stingray-tracking-devices-whos-got-them

41. https://www.upenn.edu/gazette/0107/gaz09.html

Part Two: Big Brother and the Emergence of Surveillance Capitalism

1. https://openlibrary.org/works/OL109098W/First_part_of_the_institutes_of_the_laws_of_England

2. *Wilson v. Arkansas*, 514 U.S. 927, at 932 fn. 2 citing 5 Co. Rep., at 91b, 77 Eng. Rep., at 196 (referring to 3 Edw. I, ch. 17).

3. https://www.theguardian.com/technology/2016/feb/09/internet-of-things-smart-home-devices-government-surveillance-james-clapper

4. https://www.menshealth.com/fitness/a19853443/i-used-a-fitness
   -tracker-to-track-my-activity-level-during-sex/
5. https://splinternews.com/fitbit-data-just-undermined-a-womans-rape
   -claim-1793848735
6. https://www.myrental.com/about-us and previous disclosures on the
   same site collected on June 19, 2019, by #REPRESENT, a project of the
   Consumer Education Foundation at www.representconsumers.org.
7. https://www.mysmartmove.com/, accessed January 25, 2021.
8. https://www.representconsumers.org/wp-content/uploads/2020
   /04/2020.04.29_REPRESENT-Letter-to-FTC-re-Scores.pdf
9. https://www.consumeraffairs.com/finance/corelogic-saferent.html
10. https://www.representconsumers.org/wp-content/uploads/2019/06
    /2019.06.24-FTC-Letter-Surveillance-Scores.pdf
11. Ibid.
12. https://www.wsj.com/articles/the-secret-trust-scores-companies-use
    -to-judge-us-all-11554523206
13. Ibid.
14. https://www.representconsumers.org/wp-content/uploads/2019/06
    /2019.06.24-FTC-Letter-Surveillance-Scores.pdf
15. Ibid.
16. https://dpl-surveillance-equipment.com/miscellaneous/on-hold-for
    -45-minutes-it-might-be-your-secret-customer-score-gotbitcoin/
17. Ibid.
18. http://docplayer.net/151333511-Represent-re-secret-surveillance
    -scoring-urgent-request-for-investigation-and-enforcement-action.html
19. Ibid.
20. https://news.northeastern.edu/2014/10/23/ecommerce-study
21. https://www.representconsumers.org/wp-content/uploads/2019/06
    /2019.06.24-FTC-Letter-Surveillance-Scores.pdf
22. Ibid.
23. Ibid.
24. Ibid.
25. https://www.propublica.org/article/you-snooze-you-lose-insurers
    -make-the-old-adage-literally-true
26. https://www.bbc.com/news/technology-46822439
27. https://www.ftc.gov/system/files/documents/reports/data-brokers
    -call-transparency-accountability-report-federal-trade-commission
    -may-2014/140527databrokerreport.pdf
28. Ibid.
29. Ibid.

30. https://www.propublica.org/article/facebook-doesnt-tell-users -everything-it-really-knows-about-them

31. Wolfie Christl, "Corporate Surveillance in Everyday Life," Cracked Labs, June 2017, https://crackedlabs.org/en/corporate-surveillance.

32. Alexis de Tocqueville, *Democracy in America*, trans. and ed. Harvey C. Mansfield and Delba Winthrop (Chicago, IL: University of Chicago Press, 2002), 663–64.

33. A. L. Beaman et al., "Self-Awareness and Transgression in Children: Two Field Studies," *Journal of Personality and Social Psychology* 37, no. 10 (1979): 1835–46, https://doi.org/10.1037/0022-3514.37.10.1835.

34. Cristian Damsa, MD, et al., "Heisenberg in the ER: Observation Appears to Reduce Involuntary Intramuscular Injections in a Psychiatric Emergency Service," *General Hospital Psychiatry* 28, issue 5 (September–October 2006): 431–33.

35. Daniel Nettle, Kenneth Nott, Melissa Bateson, "'Cycle Thieves, We Are Watching You': Impact of a Simple Signage Intervention Against Bicycle Theft," *PLoS ONE* 7, no. 12 (2012): e51738, https://doi.org/10.1371 /journal.pone.0051738.

36. Melissa Bateson et al., "Do Images of 'Watching Eyes' Induce Behaviour That Is More Pro-Social or More Normative? A Field Experiment on Littering," *PLoS ONE* 8, no. 12 (2013): e82055, https://doi.org /10.1371/journal.pone.0082055.

37. https://www.pillarcatholic.com/p/pillar-investigates-usccb-gen-sec

38. https://www.tijmenschep.com/about/

39. https://www.socialcooling.com/

40. Lizette Alvarez, "Spring Break Gets Tamer as World Watches Online," *New York Times*, March 16, 2012, https://www.nytimes.com/2012/03 /16/us/spring-break-gets-tamer-as-world-watches-online.html.

41. https://www.socialcooling.com/

42. https://www.nytimes.com/1994/10/21/business/2d-look-at-prime -time-rule.html

Part Three: Big Brother and the Real Global Info Wars

1. https://www.smithsonianmag.com/history/richard-clarke-on-who -was-behind-the-stuxnet-attack-160630516/

2. https://www.hsdl.org/?view&did=757312

3. https://www.wsj.com/articles/iranian-hackers-infiltrated-new-york -dam-in-2013-1450662559

4. https://www.bloomberg.com/news/articles/2020-01-05/iranian -attack-on-adelson-provides-lesson-on-cyber-strategy

5. https://www.nytimes.com/2013/02/13/us/executive-order-on-cybersecurity-is-issued.html

6. Ibid.

7. Nicole Perlroth, *This Is How They Tell Me the World Ends: The Cyberweapons Arms Race* (New York: Bloomsbury Publishing, 2020).

8. Perlroth, *This Is How They Tell Me the World Ends.*

9. Kim Zetter, "Inside the Cunning, Unprecedented Hack of Ukraine's Power Grid," *Wired*, March 3, 2016, https://www.wired.com/2016/03/inside-cunning-unprecedented-hack-ukraines-power-grid/.

10. https://apnews.com/article/hacking-russia-estonia-e931e674091b080f7a01642b01729bbe

11. Andy Greenberg, "The Untold Story of NotPetya, the Most Devastating Cyberattack in History," *Wired*, August 22, 2018, https://www.wired.com/story/notpetya-cyberattack-ukraine-russia-code-crashed-the-world/.

12. https://twitter.com/MarkWarner/status/996434167515828224

13. https://www.politico.com/story/2018/05/15/white-house-eliminates-cyber-adviser-post-542916

14. https://www.nytimes.com/2020/12/13/us/politics/russian-hackers-us-government-treasury-commerce.html

15. https://www.nytimes.com/2020/11/17/us/politics/trump-fires-christopher-krebs.html

16. https://www.nbcnews.com/politics/white-house/trump-downplays-russia-hack-first-comments-massive-breach-implicates-china-n1251813

17. https://apnews.com/article/donald-trump-politics-mark-levin-coronavirus-pandemic-hacking-6080f156125a4a46edef2a6dcf826611

18. Ibid.

19. https://www.msn.com/en-us/news/politics/the-white-house-was-set-to-accuse-russia-of-the-devastating-cyberattack-on-the-us-government-s-computer-systems-but-was-told-at-the-last-minute-to-stand-down/ar-BB1c57Lx

20. Wilson Bryan Key, *Subliminal Seduction: Are You Being Sexually Aroused by This Picture?* (New York: Signet Books, 19th Printing Ed., 1974).

21. https://www.snopes.com/fact-check/subliminal-advertising/

22. Shoshana Zuboff, *The Age of Surveillance Capitalism: The Fight for a Human Future at the New Frontier of Power* (New York: PublicAffairs, 2019).

23. https://www.nscai.gov/2021-final-report/

24. https://www.axios.com/newsletters/axios-future-109540a0-6454-40fd-b380-14798db38a48.html?utm_source=newsletter&utm_medium=email&utm_campaign=newsletter_axiosfutureofwork&stream=future

25. https://www.nytimes.com/2021/07/25/world/europe/disinformation
-social-media.html/

26. It was reprinted, for example, by *The Guardian*, https://www.theguardian
.com/commentisfree/2021/jul/15/theres-a-new-tactic-for-exposing
-you-to-radical-content-online-the-slow-red-pill/

27. https://donotresearch.net/posts/memetic-tactics-the-slow-red-pill

28. https://www.reuters.com/investigates/special-report/usa-riteaid
-software/

29. https://www.nytimes.com/interactive/2021/03/18/magazine/facial
-recognition-clearview-ai.html

30. https://www.nytimes.com/interactive/2020/07/03/us/george-floyd
-protests-crowd-size.html

31. https://www.documentcloud.org/documents/4412917-FBI
-Intelligence-Report-Tracking-Black-Lives.html

32. https://theintercept.com/2018/03/19/black-lives-matter-fbi
-surveillance/

33. https://docs.microsoft.com/en-us/xamarin/xamarin-forms/data
-cloud/azure-cognitive-services/emotion-recognition

34. https://www.nytimes.com/interactive/2021/03/18/magazine/facial
-recognition-clearview-ai.html

35. https://www.wired.com/story/china-social-credit-score-system/

36. https://www.nytimes.com/interactive/2021/03/18/magazine/facial
-recognition-clearview-ai.html

37. https://www.theguardian.com/business/2020/dec/17/alibaba
-offered-clients-facial-recognition-to-identify-uighur-people

38. Ibid.

39. https://www.cbsnews.com/news/ok-youve-deleted-facebook-but-is
-your-data-still-out-there/

40. https://www.youtube.com/embed/LGiiQUMaShw

41. https://www.cnbc.com/2017/10/04/scott-galloway-russia
-weaponizing-facebook-is-a-tipping-point-in-tech.html

42. https://harpers.org/archive/2016/04/legalize-it-all/

43. https://www.nbcnews.com/tech/social-media/klamath-falls-oregon
-victory-declared-over-antifa-which-never-showed-n1226681

44. https://www.theverge.com/2020/6/5/21281581/antifa-bus-hoax
-trump-misinformation-protests-police

45. https://www.cbsnews.com/news/tucker-carlson-fox-news-advertisers
-leave-anti-racism-comments/

46. https://www.washingtonpost.com/news/monkey-cage/wp/2017/09/14/5-things-you-need-to-know-about-rohingya-crisis-and-how-it-could-roil-southeast-asia/
47. https://www.ft.com/content/21d5f650-1e6a-11e7-a454-ab04428977f9
48. https://www.farmlandgrab.org/post/view/26876-posco-daewoo-launches-agribusiness-in-myanmar
49. https://www.mmtimes.com/opinion/22240-japan-set-to-reap-returns-on-investment-in-myanmar.html
50. https://www.nytimes.com/2018/10/15/technology/myanmar-facebook-genocide.html
51. Ibid.
52. https://www.nytimes.com/2018/08/25/world/asia/rohingya-myanmar-ethnic-cleansing-anniversary.html
53. https://www.nytimes.com/2018/07/07/world/asia/myanmar-rohingya-rape-refugees-childbirth.html
54. https://www.nytimes.com/2018/10/15/technology/myanmar-facebook-genocide.html

Part Four: Putting the Reins on Surveillance Capitalism

1. https://www.aclu-il.org/en/biometric-information-privacy-act-bipa
2. https://apnews.com/article/technology-business-san-francisco-chicago-lawsuits-af6b42212e43be1b63b5c290eb5bfd85
3. https://www.nytimes.com/2020/06/24/technology/facial-recognition-arrest.html
4. https://www.merkley.senate.gov/news/press-releases/merkley-colleagues-introduce-legislation-to-ban-government-use-of-facial-recognition-and-other-biometric-technology-2020
5. https://www.merkley.senate.gov/news/press-releases/merkley-booker-introduce-legislation-to-prohibit-irresponsible-government-use-of-facial-recognition-technology-2020
6. https://www.theguardian.com/technology/2014/may/13/spain-everyman-google-mario-costeja-gonzalez
7. The gdpr.eu website is not official but is operated by Proton Technologies AG, which is cofunded by Project REP-791727-1 of the Horizon 2020 Framework Programme of the European Union.
8. https://gdpr.eu/what-is-gdpr/
9. https://www.europarl.europa.eu/charter/pdf/text_en.pdf

10. https://www.cambridge.org/core/journals/german-law-journal/article/essence-of-the-fundamental-rights-to-privacy-and-data-protection-finding-the-way-through-the-maze-of-the-cjeus-constitutional-reasoning/00621C26FA14CCD55AD0B4F4AD38ED09

11. https://termly.io/resources/articles/gdpr-for-dummies/

12 Ibid.

13. https://www.washingtonpost.com/news/volokh-conspiracy/wp/2017/03/15/n-y-bill-would-require-people-to-remove-inaccurate-irrelevant-inadequate-or-excessive-statements-about-others/

14. https://www.pewresearch.org/fact-tank/2020/01/27/most-americans-support-right-to-have-some-personal-info-removed-from-online-searches/

15. https://www.cnet.com/features/porn-addiction-is-ruining-lives-but-scientists-arent-convinced-its-real/

16. https://www.yourbrainonporn.com/relevant-research-and-articles-about-the-studies/porn-use-sex-addiction-studies/studies-find-escalation-and-habituation-in-porn-users-tolerance/

17. Norman Doidge, *The Brain That Changes Itself: Stories of Personal Triumph from the Frontiers of Brain Science* (New York: Penguin, 2007).

18. Derek O'Callaghan, Derek Greene, Maura Conway (lead authors), "Down the (White) Rabbit Hole: The Extreme Right and Online Recommender Systems," *Social Science Computer Review*, October 16, 2014, https://journals.sagepub.com/doi/10.1177/0894439314555329.

19. Zeynep Tufekci, "YouTube, the Great Radicalizer," *New York Times*, March 10, 2018, https://www.nytimes.com/2018/03/10/opinion/sunday/youtube-politics-radical.html

20. https://www.policemag.com/592586/140-officers-were-injured-in-capitol-riot-officials-say

21. https://www.cnbc.com/2021/03/08/23-house-dems-ask-facebook-about-weapons-ads-in-wake-of-jan-6.html

22. https://www.npr.org/2015/03/02/390245038/ben-franklins-famous-liberty-safety-quote-lost-its-context-in-21st-century

23. Fritz Thyssen, *I Paid Hitler* (New York: Farrar & Rinehart, 1941).

24. https://www.nytimes.com/1944/04/09/archives/wallace-defines-american-fascism-the-vice-president-says-it.html

25. https://www.wyden.senate.gov/imo/media/doc/The%20Fourth%20Amendment%20Is%20Not%20For%20Sale%20Act%20of%202021%20Bill%20Text.pdf

26. https://www.dw.com/en/hello-big-brother-how-china-controls-its
-citizens-through-social-media/a-38243388

27. https://bpr.berkeley.edu/2018/10/24/wechat-isnt-chinas-facebook
-its-something-bigger/

28. https://nca.tandfonline.com/doi/abs/10.1080/17544750.2019
.1583261?journalCode=rcjc20

29. https://www.cultofmac.com/430097/in-china-taobao-is-like-amazon
-but-bigger-and-faster/

30. https://www.scmp.com/economy/china-economy/article/3019333
/chinas-social-credit-system-will-not-lead-citizens-losing

31. https://www.businessinsider.com/china-social-credit-system
-punishments-and-rewards-explained-2018-4?op=1

32. https://www.independent.co.uk/news/world/asia/china-surveillance
-big-data-score-censorship-a7375221.html

33. https://fortune.com/2020/11/03/china-surveillance-system-backlash
-worlds-largest/

34. https://www.nytimes.com/2013/03/10/business/in-a-changing
-china-new-matchmaking-markets.html

35. https://chinacopyrightandmedia.wordpress.com/2014/06/14
/planning-outline-for-the-construction-of-a-social-credit-system-2014
-2020/

36. https://uschinatoday.org/features/2020/07/14/chinas-social-credit
-score/

37. Christopher Wylie, *Mindf*ck: Cambridge Analytica and the Plot to Break
America* (New York: Random House, 2019).

38. https://www.businessinsider.com/google-users-locked-out-after-years
-2020-10?op=1

39. https://twitter.com/miguelytob/status/1315749803041619981

40. https://www.sgtreport.com/2021/08/fbis-whitmer-kidnapping-plot
-from-bad-to-worse-viva-frei-vlawg/

ACKNOWLEDGMENTS

Special thanks go to Troy N. Miller, who worked with me for years as a producer and writer for the television show *The Big Picture*, which I hosted every weeknight for seven years in Washington, DC. Troy worked hard as a researcher, sounding board, and editor, and deserves recognition for it.

At Berrett-Koehler Publishers, Steve Piersanti—who was the founder—worked with me to kick off this series. It's been a labor of love for both of us, and I'm so grateful to Steve for his insights, rigor, and passion for this project. Of the many other people at BK who have helped with this book (and some projects associated with it), special thanks to Jeevan Sivasubramaniam (who has helped keep me sane for years) and Neal Maillet, a constant source of encouragement and wisdom. BK is an extraordinary publishing company, and it's been an honor to have them publish my books for almost two decades. And thanks to Tai Moses, who edited my *Thom Hartmann Reader* and returned to do a first pass with this book, for all her insights and help.

BK also provided a brilliant final editor for the book, Elissa Rabellino, who did a great job smoothing and tightening the text.

Bill Gladstone, my agent for over two decades, helped make this book—and the *Hidden History* series—possible. Bill is truly one of the best in the business.

My executive producer, Shawn Taylor, helped with booking expert guests on my radio and TV programs, many of whom provided great information and anecdotes for this book. And my video producer, Nate Atwell, is a true visual genius. I'm blessed to have such a great team helping me produce a daily radio and TV program, which supports my writing work.

And, as always, my best sounding board, editor, and friend is my wife, Louise. Without her, in all probability none of my books would ever have seen the light of day.

INDEX

ABOUT THE AUTHOR

© Ian Sbalcio

Thom Hartmann is a four-time Project Censored Award–winning, *New York Times* best-selling author and America's number one progressive talk show host. He and his wife, Louise, live with three cats and two dogs on the Columbia River in Portland, Oregon.

BOOKS BY THOM HARTMANN

Berrett–Koehler
Publishers

Berrett-Koehler is an independent publisher dedicated to an ambitious mission: *Connecting people and ideas to create a world that works for all.*

Our publications span many formats, including print, digital, audio, and video. We also offer online resources, training, and gatherings. And we will continue expanding our products and services to advance our mission.

We believe that the solutions to the world's problems will come from all of us, working at all levels: in our society, in our organizations, and in our own lives. Our publications and resources offer pathways to creating a more just, equitable, and sustainable society. They help people make their organizations more humane, democratic, diverse, and effective (and we don't think there's any contradiction there). And they guide people in creating positive change in their own lives and aligning their personal practices with their aspirations for a better world.

And we strive to practice what we preach through what we call "The BK Way." At the core of this approach is *stewardship,* a deep sense of responsibility to administer the company for the benefit of all of our stakeholder groups, including authors, customers, employees, investors, service providers, sales partners, and the communities and environment around us. Everything we do is built around stewardship and our other core values of *quality, partnership, inclusion,* and *sustainability.*

This is why Berrett-Koehler is the first book publishing company to be both a B Corporation (a rigorous certification) and a benefit corporation (a for-profit legal status), which together require us to adhere to the highest standards for corporate, social, and environmental performance. And it is why we have instituted many pioneering practices (which you can learn about at www.bkconnection.com), including the Berrett-Koehler Constitution, the Bill of Rights and Responsibilities for BK Authors, and our unique Author Days.

We are grateful to our readers, authors, and other friends who are supporting our mission. We ask you to share with us examples of how BK publications and resources are making a difference in your lives, organizations, and communities at www.bkconnection.com/impact.

Dear reader,

Thank you for picking up this book and welcome to the worldwide BK community! You're joining a special group of people who have come together to create positive change in their lives, organizations, and communities.

What's BK all about?

Our mission is to connect people and ideas to create a world that works for all.

Why? Our communities, organizations, and lives get bogged down by old paradigms of self-interest, exclusion, hierarchy, and privilege. But we believe that can change. That's why we seek the leading experts on these challenges—and share their actionable ideas with you.

A welcome gift

To help you get started, we'd like to offer you a free copy of one of our bestselling ebooks:

www.bkconnection.com/welcome

When you claim your **free ebook,** you'll also be subscribed to our blog.

Our freshest insights

Access the best new tools and ideas for leaders at all levels on our blog at ideas.bkconnection.com.

Sincerely,

Your friends at Berrett-Koehler